D1186832

CONTENTS

Written by Richard Marson

BBC
Blue Peter
Annual 2007

Pedigree®

Published by Pedigree Books Limited, Beach Hill House, Walnut Gardens, Exeter, Devon, EX4 4DH.
Email: books@pedigreegroup.co.uk By arrangement with the BBC.

£7.99

Hello

And welcome to Blue Peter's thirty-sixth book. Another year has rushed past and, as ever, it has been a tough job to choose what to include and what to leave out.

As well as the best of our stories, competitions, cooks and makes, on this page you can see some of our favourite moments from the past twelve months. Why not see how many you recognize and then look up the answers on page 109?

There's been a lot to get excited about this year. The success of our Treasure Trail Appeal for Childline was a high point. Thanks to your hard work we reached over four times our original target. Blue Peter viewers really are the best and you prove it time and time again – whether it is taking part in the Appeal, entering our competitions or getting in touch with ideas, drawings, stories, poems and recipes. Every week, we get thousands of emails and letters. We love finding out what you're into and what you think and awarding badges for your efforts. While we're talking big numbers, the Blue Peter website gets over two million hits a week and we've got exciting plans to make it better and better, so why not join us online? You can find us at bbc.co.uk/cbbc/bluepeter. That will keep you fully up-to-date with all our news and plans.

It has been a year with lots of news and a few important comings and goings.

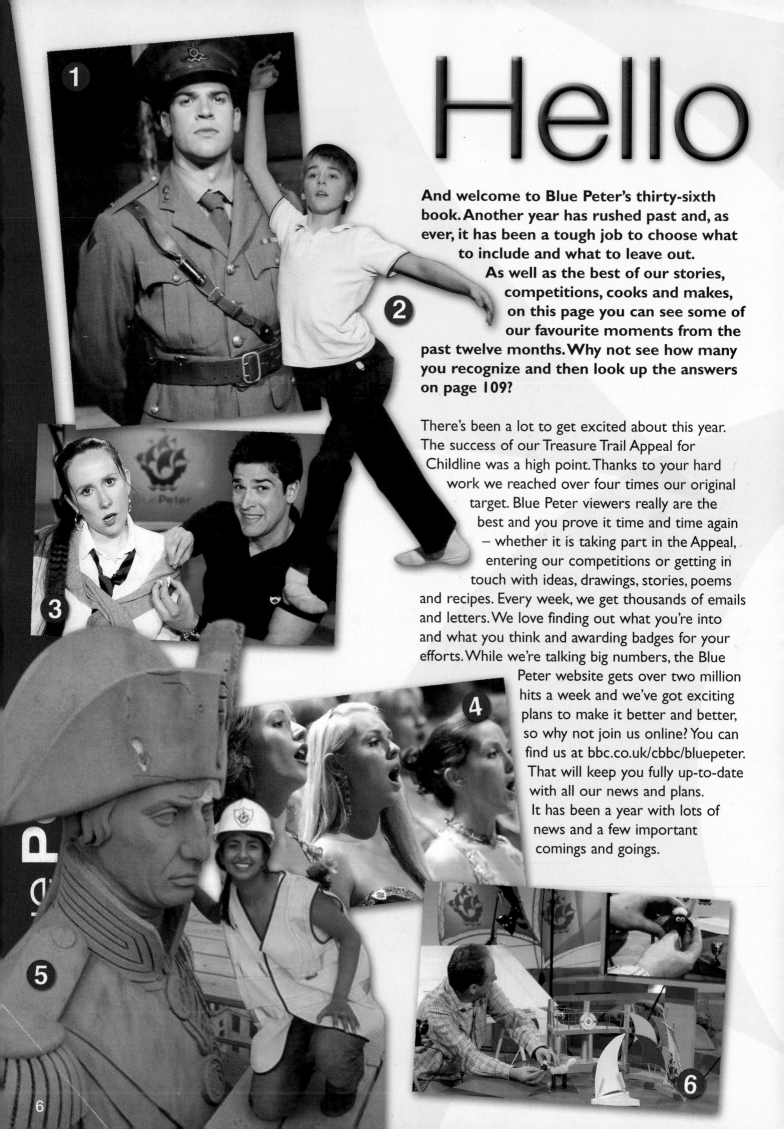

There!

The first was the very sad and totally unexpected death of Smudge, who had only been on the programme for ten months. He was run over near his home and the tragedy happened just too late to be included in last year's book. We wanted to wait a while before finding a new cat but eventually, a few months later, Socks arrived. You can read all about him on page 74.

Saying goodbye to really good friends is always hard and this year we've said farewell to two of the very best – Liz and Matt. On page 92, you can see our special tribute to both of them.

Meanwhile, finding our new boy, Andy Akinwolere, meant searching the length and breadth of Britain, looking for the right person to join the team in time for our next season. You can read about Andy's audition on page 102. We hope you'll enjoy getting to know him and that you'll follow all our adventures over the months to come.

Zoe   Karine xxx

Blue Peter

7

TRY HARD

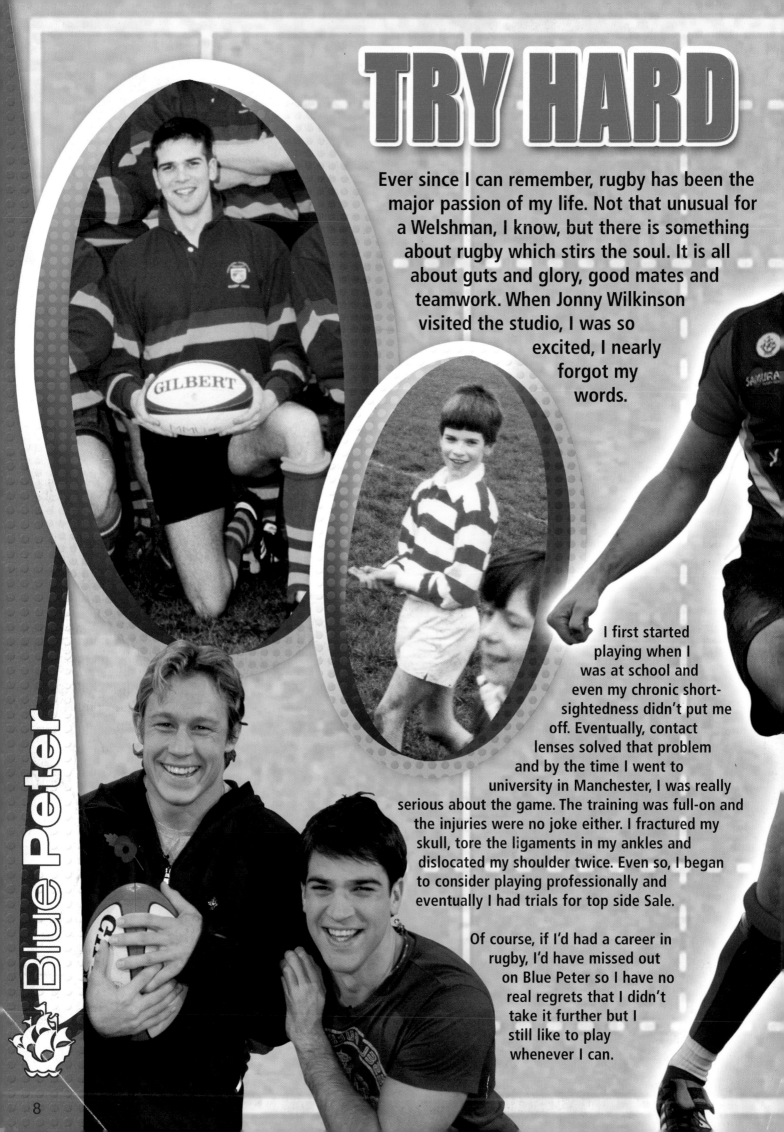

Ever since I can remember, rugby has been the major passion of my life. Not that unusual for a Welshman, I know, but there is something about rugby which stirs the soul. It is all about guts and glory, good mates and teamwork. When Jonny Wilkinson visited the studio, I was so excited, I nearly forgot my words.

I first started playing when I was at school and even my chronic short-sightedness didn't put me off. Eventually, contact lenses solved that problem and by the time I went to university in Manchester, I was really serious about the game. The training was full-on and the injuries were no joke either. I fractured my skull, tore the ligaments in my ankles and dislocated my shoulder twice. Even so, I began to consider playing professionally and eventually I had trials for top side Sale.

Of course, if I'd had a career in rugby, I'd have missed out on Blue Peter so I have no real regrets that I didn't take it further but I still like to play whenever I can.

Blue Peter

Recently, when I was back home in Cardiff I took Blue Peter cameras with me to follow the action as I rejoined my old team, a Welsh-speaking side called Clwb Rygbi Cymry Caerdydd. My usual position is number nine or scrum-half but today I was asked to play number fifteen or full-back. We were up against a team called Caerau Ely, who are well-known for playing hard, so I knew it wasn't going to be a picnic.

The whistle went, the ball was kicked and I forgot all about the cameras and just went for it. Eighty minutes later, it was all over. The score? Ely, 29. Cymry Caerdydd, 26. We'd lost and I was gutted, even though I'd enjoyed every moment out there.

Blue Peter

When I was growing up, my Dad and I often used to go to Cardiff Arms Park to watch my local side, one of the best teams in Wales, the Cardiff Blues. They were my heroes, so it was a special moment when I discovered that they'd invited me to join one of their regular training sessions. I weigh about 85kg but you wouldn't have thought so considering the ease with which the players threw me into the air during the line-out.

One of them, Jamie Robinson, was actually in my class at school so it was a bit of a reunion – right down to the moment when I was busy talking to our camera crew and the team crept up behind me and pulled down my trackie bottoms!

Blue Peter

One real highlight of
the session was the chance to
meet Blues player and rugby legend
Jonah Lomu. Jonah shook my hand and beamed. He seemed
very friendly in fact – until he agreed to let me tackle
him. The smile vanished as I charged towards him.
As I made contact, my shoulder felt like it had
been rammed into my hip. Even then he was only
using about half of his usual strength.

Rugby certainly isn't a game for the faint-
hearted. But take it from me, if you get the chance to
play, although it may mean braving the cold, plenty of
mud and a few bruises, I don't think there is any sport
which can beat it for total team spirit and sheer
exhilaration.

Blue Pete

ALL THE QUEEN'S HORSES

One thing I won't miss about **Blue Peter** is the journey to work. I live out in the country and getting to our studios on time always meant an early start. The advantage of any early start is that the roads are never as busy. Unless, that is, you get stuck behind a convoy of army horses and riders.

This happens more often than you might think because the park just up the road from the BBC is where the King's Troop of the Royal Horse Artillery regularly take their horses for an early morning exercise and training session. It's a breathtaking spectacle on a misty winter morning but it does slow down the traffic! I was curious to find out what they actually got up to there and why, so, on the theory of "if you can't beat them, join them", I looked out my riding boots and reported to the King's Troop barracks in north London, home to 136 magnificent horses.

Military horsemanship demands the highest possible standards. Soldiers are trained in every aspect of equine care – as I found out when I helped a King's Troop farrier or blacksmith to make some horseshoes. The wear and tear from pounding the London streets mean the horses need new shoes far more often than usual. This is not a job to try if you enjoy a lie-in. In the stables, I mucked out, groomed and saddled up my horse with its highly polished army saddle but it was still before dawn by the time we'd finished and were finally ready to ride out on to the London streets.

The horses take part in lots of ceremonial exercises and it's important for them to get used to cars, pedestrians and all the unexpected noise and bustle of city life. It was an unusual and exhilarating feeling to ride through London's streets and to see the reaction from drivers and passers-by.

We arrived at the park for the main task of the day – a full rehearsal of the drill the horses would go through for the Queen's birthday salute. It takes six horses to pull one of the massive guns and the skill of both horse and rider is vital to ensure the whole exercise runs smoothly.

They even rehearse the firing of the cannon salute. The noise was staggering. The whole morning had been hard work but great fun. My first job after leaving Blue Peter was Sport Relief's celebrity showjumping programme, Only Fools On Horses. The King's Troop very kindly gave me some extra riding lessons to prepare for it and I can't thank them enough.

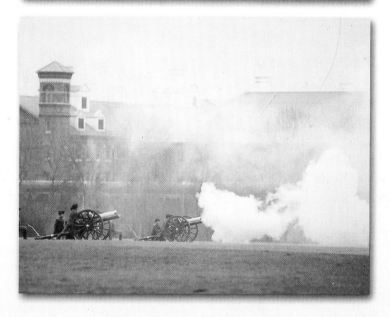

TOTALLY BLUE PETER

Totally Blue Peter was our all-singing, all-dancing Christmas spectacular. It took us back to 1980s New York which meant big hair, big shoulders and lots of over-the-top acting! The hero was a sweet-natured guy called Joey Jones and he tells the story.

I'm Joey. Dreaming of becoming a singer, but stuck behind the counter of a downtown coffee shop.

Meet my best friend – Dee Dee, whose job as PA to the Editor of the glossy Blue Peter fashion magazine kept her very busy, 24/7.

Cassie Carrington was her boss. Editor of Blue Peter and Queen of Mean.

Dee Dee had all the ideas but Cassie took the credit.

LOUD-MOUTH

I had my own problems. The coffee shop where I worked was run by a loud-mouth called Maria Bonetti. She was never off my case.

Things got serious when Dee Dee discovered that Cassie was plotting to ruin Blue Peter magazine's all important Christmas issue and join its arch rival, Hiya!

I persuaded Dee Dee to break into Cassie's office one night to find evidence of her treachery.

We were nearly caught but somehow Dee Dee managed to persuade Cassie that I had the right looks to be Blue Peter magazine's Christmas cover star.

I wasn't so sure. I wanted to be a singer not a model. But hey – if it was Cassie's plan to ruin the magazine, maybe she figured my face on the front page would do the trick.

Dee Dee took me to her old pal, the outrageous stylist Ricco. He told me I had good skin, good eyes and good cheekbones and that by the time he was finished with me, all the girls would want to date me and all the guys would want to be me.

So I quit the coffee shop and gave it a go – what do you reckon?

Meanwhile, we realised we needed to get our evidence to Blue Peter's big cheese, Mac Mackenzie. He was throwing a party so I got a job as a waiter there.

Unfortunately, Cassie spotted me and guessed what was up.

HENCHMAN

She got her henchman to tie me up, out of the way.

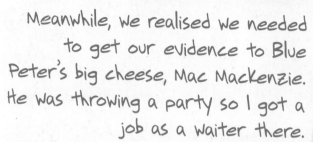

But she reckoned without Dee Dee who told Mac everything. I freed myself just in time to hear him publicly exposing Cassie for the viper she really was.

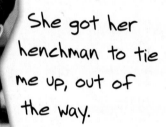

And that was about it. I got my break as a singer. Dee Dee got Cassie's job. And Dee Dee and me admitted we were more than just friends - and got married! I guess it was a Christmas none of us would forget in a hurry.....

Totally Blue Peter was our most ambitious Christmas entertainment in years. It took weeks of planning, rehearsing and filming with lots of dance routines, costume changes and two different parts for multi-talented Matt. We hope you enjoyed it as much as we did!

Flying Angels

These angels make perfect mobiles as well as pretty decorations for a Christmas tree.

1. To make the angels you will need some thin card or stiff paper. Draw a circle on the card using a medium-sized dinner plate for a pattern. Cut out the circle.

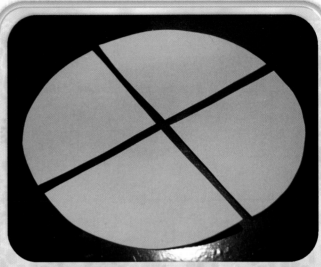

2. Fold the circle in half twice, pressing firmly along the folds. Open out the circle and cut along the folded lines. You will be left with 4 quarter circles which will make 4 angels.

3. To make one angel's gown, fold a quarter circle in half, matching up the straight edges. For the head draw around a 2p coin on coloured card and then cut out the circle.
Glue the head over the point at the top of the gown.

4. For the wings cut 2 oblongs of paper about 10 x 7 cm in size. Thin, lined writing paper is ideal for this. Make small pleats, starting at a narrow end and folding on the lines, backwards and forwards to the other end of the paper, like making a fan. Holding the pleats together, cut one end into a point.
Make a second wing and join the two together with sticky tape at the straight end.
Spread glue all along the straight inside edges of the gown. Put the taped ends of the wings inside the gown just below the head and press the glued edges together to hold the wings in place.

5 Cut out 2 sleeve shapes to match the gown and glue on simple hand shapes cut from the same card as the face. Glue the tops of the sleeves either side of the angle with the hands and ends of the sleeves overlapping the gown at the front.

6 Glue a little tinsel on the back of the head. To create a halo, dab a little glue around the front of the head and fold over some of the strands onto the glue. Press hard to make sure the strands stick and trim any long ones which cover the face too much.

7 Draw on eyes and a smiley mouth. Spread out the wings as far as possible and decorate the hem and cuffs of the angel's gown with glitter.

8 To enable you to hang up your angel, take a length of sewing thread and sew it through the top of the head or fix to the back of the tinsel hair with a tiny piece of sticky tape.

After Christmas, fold the wings and put the angels away until next year.

WINTER SAFARI

I started my safari just as the January days were at their coldest, darkest and most bitter and it was the perfect antidote to the British winter.

My first assignment was to help the AfriCat Foundation, who work hard to prevent the killing of endangered big cats like leopards and cheetahs. Without their work, these unique animals might be extinct within just 50 years.

Any injured or orphaned leopards like this one are treated and then released back into the wild but not before they have been fitted with radio collars so that AfriCat can track them and make sure they continue to do well.

TO NAMIBIA

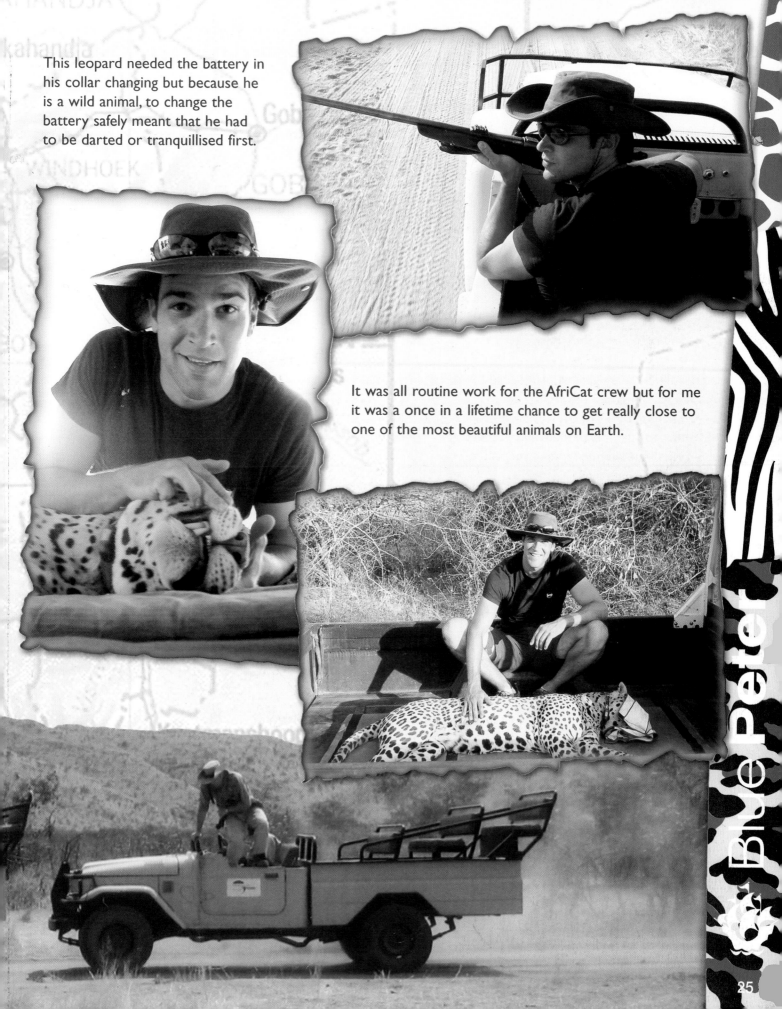

This leopard needed the battery in his collar changing but because he is a wild animal, to change the battery safely meant that he had to be darted or tranquillised first.

It was all routine work for the AfriCat crew but for me it was a once in a lifetime chance to get really close to one of the most beautiful animals on Earth.

Blue Peter

After my close encounter with the leopard, I set off to explore the vast Namib desert, the driest land known to man and yet the richest source of diamonds on the planet. This explains why so many explorers and settlers have ventured out here over the years but there are huge risks for the unwary traveller. It's blisteringly hot and five years can pass without a drop of water falling from the sky. You can all too easily get lost and disorientated as mile upon mile of sun-baked sand stretch around you in all directions. Countless people have lost their lives here among the biggest sand dunes on Earth. The diamonds of the desert come at a price.

Sea lions may not be the kind of animal you'd expect to find in Africa but in Pelican Point on Namibia's skeleton coast there are about 2000 of them. They're cape fur seals, to be precise, all drawn here by the plentiful supply of fish.

Taking to the sea in a canoe, I took an unforgettable closer look at these fabulous animals. It was great to know that around 1000 seal pups are born and learn to swim here every year.

The Spitzkoppe or 'pointed hill' juts 1,784 metres out from the flat Namibian plains and I was given the chance to climb it under the guidance of expert Ian Walker. It was tough and exhausting but just look at the view.

Namibia is one of the jewels of Africa and I felt lucky to have had the chance to experience some of its awesome beauty and the wonder of its wildlife.

Be A BLUE

We're looking for a very important person and it could be you! Do you want to visit the Blue Peter studio in London for a once-in-a-lifetime day out? Do you want to meet all of us, the pets and the production team? Have your photograph taken to prove it?

The photos might appear in next year's Annual just like these of last year's competition winner, 9-year-old Rachel Bedlow from Reading. She had a brilliant time as our V.I.P. and met everyone from the presenters to the pets.

As well as her exclusive look behind the scenes, she took a trip to the Blue Peter garden and afterwards she told us it was a day she'd never forget.

PETER V.I.P

Now it might be your turn. Have a look at this photograph. It was taken on the day we had a group of golden retrievers just like Lucy in the Blue Peter garden. You'll need to study it hard because we want you to spot which one is Lucy. If you don't want to spoil your Annual, just photocopy this page and draw a big circle round the dog you think is Lucy. Then send it, together with your name, age, address and telephone number to:

Blue Peter Day Out
BBC Television Centre
London W12 7RJ

The winner will be invited to be our V.I.P. for a day and what's more, we'll pay the transport for a friend and family too (up to a maximum of four people). Competition entries must be received by 28th February 2007. The winner will then be notified no later than 30th April 2007 and a date for your V.I.P. visit agreed.

RULES:

1. Entrants must be under 16.

2. One winner will be chosen at random from the correct entries and will be notified by post.

3. The judges' decision is final and no correspondence can be entered into.

4. Employees (and their relatives) of the BBC and Pedigree are not eligible to enter.

5. The competition is open to residents of the U.K., Ireland and the Channel Islands.

6. The publishers reserve the right to vary the prize, subject to availability.

Blue Peter

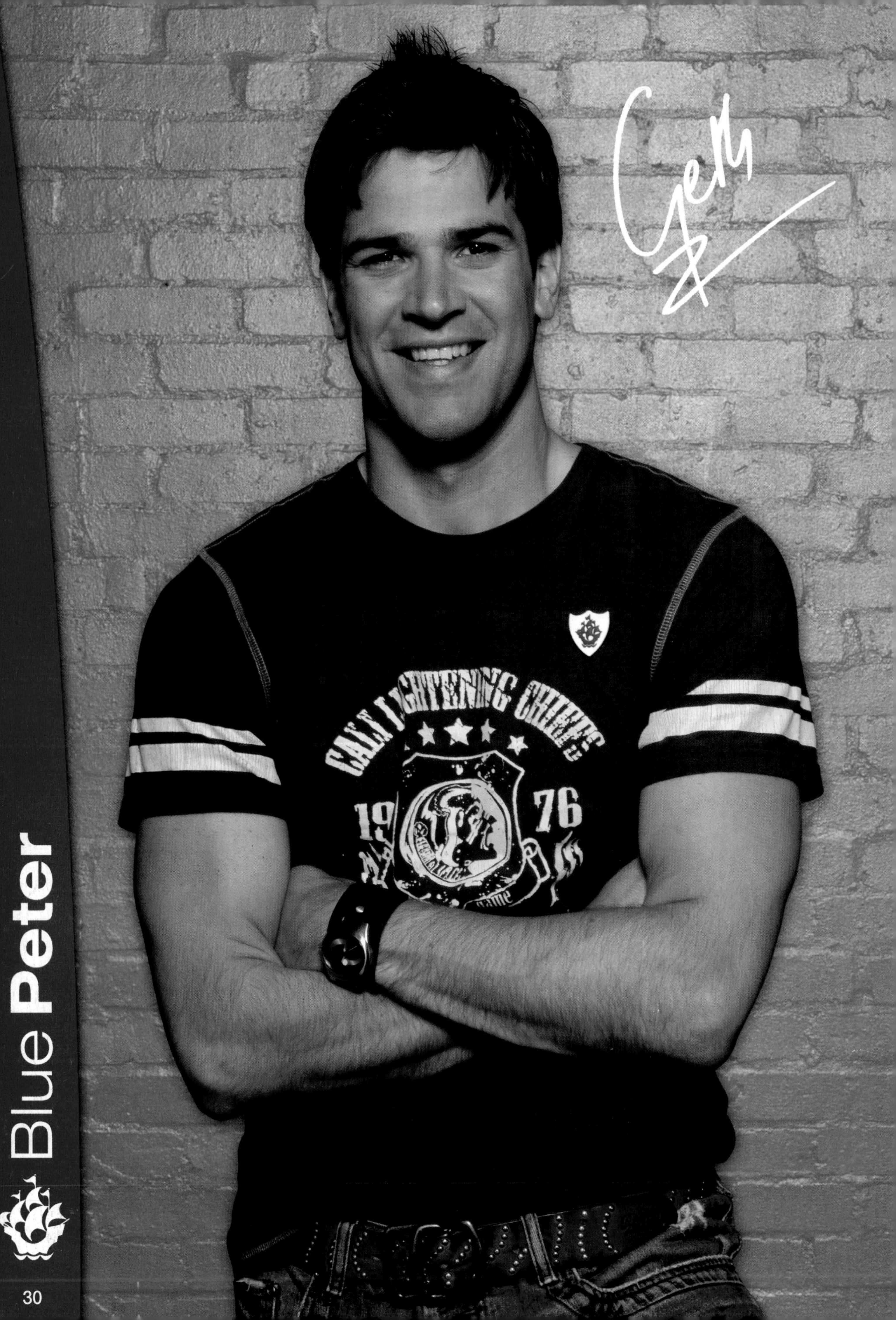

Blue Peter

Gethin Jones

I'm often asked if working on Blue Peter is as exhausting as it sometimes looks and I usually reply, "Of course but there'll be plenty of time to rest when I'm old!". No day is ever the same. For instance, over New Year, when most people were partying with friends and family, I flew off to the slopes of St. Moritz in Switzerland to take on a once-in-a-lifetime and highly dangerous challenge, the world-famous Cresta Run.

This is a super-charged downhill track carved out of the ice. The racers lie head-first on toboggans called skeletons and hurtle down the 1200-metre track at speeds of up to 90 miles an hour only centimetres above the ground. For one day only, I was going to be one of them. The padding I was given looked ancient and other than that and my helmet, there would be nothing between me the ice. It didn't help that the beginners' group I'd joined were given something traditionally called the 'death talk'. It's called that because there are very real risks of serious injuries on the Cresta run. Most of the regulars have broken lots of bones over the years. There is no practice and no way to stop once you start. You have a go and hope for the best. I was told a reasonable time to complete the course would be 70 seconds.

Heart pounding with fear, padded up and with nowhere to go but down, I took up my position at the start of the run.

"Jones!" commanded the voice from the tannoy system and even though my stomach lurched with fear, I knew I just had to go for it. It is hard to describe the thrill of that run, a mix of terror and sheer exhilaration. My time was 75.82 seconds. Not bad for a beginner, I was told. I was delighted and proud to have made it in one piece. After all, I wouldn't want to miss a single day of the best job in the world!

Blue Peter

31

GETH GLOVES UP

Twenty One-year-old Kevin Mitchell, nicknamed the Dagenham Destroyer, is one of Britain's brightest boxing hopes. Boxing is a sport which takes no prisoners – to succeed, you need strength, stamina and the will to win in situations where most people would give up and go home. I think it was my Commando Yomp which gave my boss, Blue Peter's Editor, the idea of sending me for a day's training with Kevin. I thought I'd prepare by putting in a bit of extra time at the gym but looking back, I really had no idea what I was letting myself in for.

I arrived bright and early, in time to join Kevin for his power breakfast – muesli and crumpets with peanut butter. Kevin's been boxing since he was 11 years old and eating properly is just part of the total discipline he accepts is the name of the game. Before we set off to his gym, he showed me one of his proudest possessions – the belt he won as super featherweight champion.

Blue Peter

32

Kevin trains seven days a week, fifty-two weeks a year. Now I enjoy keeping fit but as Kevin explained what he had lined up for me, I felt a strong urge to turn and run! I was really nervous and had already broken into a sweat. There was no way out and Kevin warned me that I'd need to "dig in" to get through it.

He was right. The next forty-five minutes passed in an ever-increasing blur of pain as Kevin pushed me to my limits through a relentless series of boxing circuits. I had to complete each of the exercises as hard and fast as possible. Nothing is better for building up the stamina a good boxer needs to last twelve rounds and triumph in the ring.

Kevin kept me hard at it, encouraging me all the time. I was determined to do the best I could but I'd never experienced anything as hardcore as this

Blue Peter

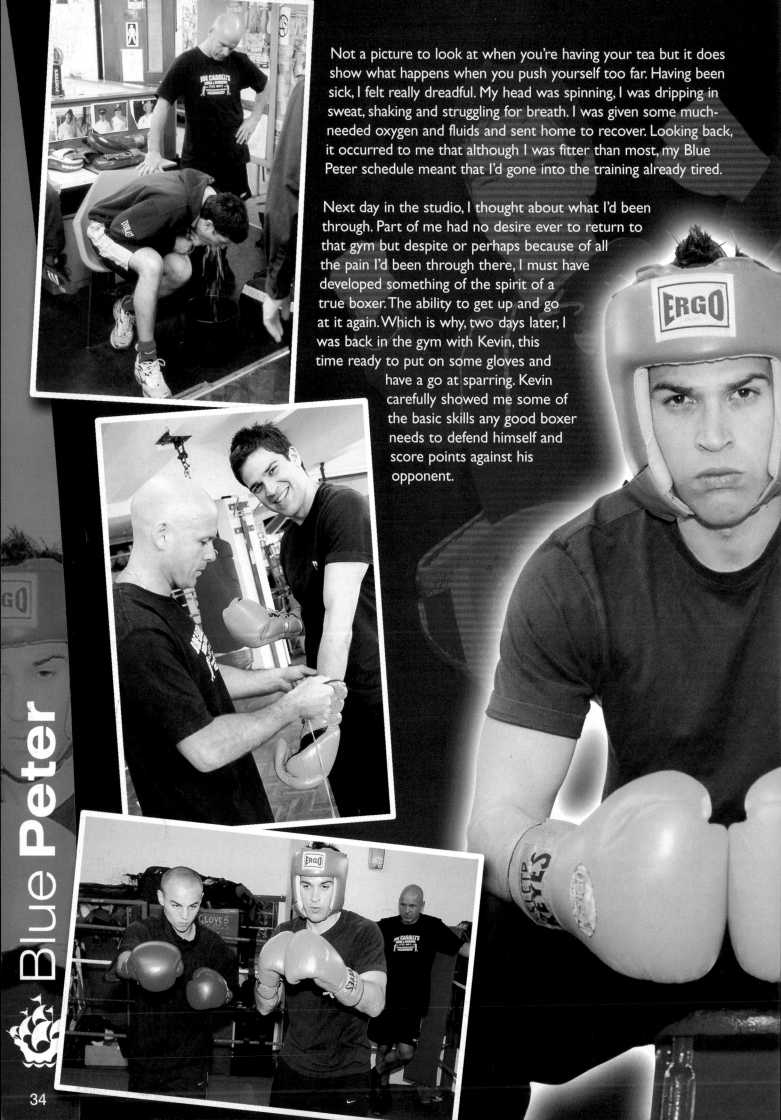

Not a picture to look at when you're having your tea but it does show what happens when you push yourself too far. Having been sick, I felt really dreadful. My head was spinning, I was dripping in sweat, shaking and struggling for breath. I was given some much-needed oxygen and fluids and sent home to recover. Looking back, it occurred to me that although I was fitter than most, my Blue Peter schedule meant that I'd gone into the training already tired.

Next day in the studio, I thought about what I'd been through. Part of me had no desire ever to return to that gym but despite or perhaps because of all the pain I'd been through there, I must have developed something of the spirit of a true boxer. The ability to get up and go at it again. Which is why, two days later, I was back in the gym with Kevin, this time ready to put on some gloves and have a go at sparring. Kevin carefully showed me some of the basic skills any good boxer needs to defend himself and score points against his opponent.

Being laced into my gloves certainly changed how I felt inside. In my imagination, I wasn't Geth from Blue Peter any more, I was Jabber Jones, the Welsh whizzkid. I didn't tell Kevin that, of course but it helped me focus as we stepped into the ring and began to spar.

Obviously, Kevin could have annihilated me in seconds if he had wanted to but instead he patiently put me through my paces and even let me score a few punches of my own. I tried not to think that I was boxing with a British champion and pretended I was squaring up to the boss instead, getting my own back in a fight I could be confident I'd win! I was soon gasping for breath again and the sparring made me realise the value of all that gym work. In the ring, the speed of your reactions is vital and your footwork is as important as what you do with your hands. Concentration and focus are all-important.

Not everybody agrees with boxing. Despite major increases in safety standards, it can be brutal and dangerous. But it also requires immense talent, real dedication and bravery which is why the government recently recommended it as an ideal sport for young people. Kevin told me that without the focus he'd got from boxing, he'd almost certainly have got into all kinds of trouble when he was growing up. I walked away from the experience with real respect for him and for anyone who decides to glove up and get in the ring.

ZARAFA

Nowadays, mainly thanks to television, most of us are used to images of the exotic wildlife found all around the world. But just imagine the sensation caused in the days when people set sight on animals like lions, tigers and giraffes for the first time.

Zarafa is Arabic for 'lovely one' and it was the name given to the very first giraffe to arrive in France 180 years ago. She was a royal gift from Emperor Muhammed Ali to King Charles X of France.

The big problem was transporting Zarafa on her 4800-kilometre journey from Ethiopia to France. She began her incredible journey on an Egyptian boat called a felucca, which carried her the length of the River Nile. Her companions were six cows, who were essential as Zarafa lived on their milk.

Then she boarded another boat to take her the rest of the way to Marseilles in France. This boat had a hole cut in the deck so that her body was in the main hold while her neck swayed up beside the mast.

Finally, 16 months after starting her incredible journey, Zarafa arrived in France. It was October 1826 and she was given a specially designed giraffe's raincoat to protect her from the autumn weather. Together with her handler Atir, she walked the 550 miles from Marseilles to Paris..

By the time she reached the capital, Zarafa had become a national sensation. She lived in a spacious purpose-built home where Atir slept by her side in a hammock so he could reach out and scratch her mane.

Fashionable women began to wear their hair 'à la giraffe', piling it as high as possible. Not be left out, men wore curious hats in the shape of Zarafa's head.

Her image was everywhere – on ties, crockery and even wallpaper.

Every month, 60,000 people flocked to visit her. People couldn't get over her unique and beautiful shape. Torchlit 'giraffe evenings' were held with Zarafa at the centre of her admiring fans. She loved the attention and was never frightened by all the fuss made of her.

There was even an outbreak of 'giraffe flu', spread by the crowds pouring into see this wonderful new animal. If they knew someone with the flu, people would ask them, "How goes the giraffe?".

Zarafa's fame never faded. When she died in 1845, 19 years after becoming the first giraffe to arrive in Paris, she was still a celebrity, visited and loved by the people of Paris, thousands of miles from the country of her birth.

Darth By Chocolate

What could be better than one of these delicious toffee and chocolate apples to snack on while watching your favourite movie? They had the Star Wars seal of approval from Darth Vader himself when he paid a visit to the studio. Actor Hayden Christensen, who plays Anakin Skywalker in the movie, even gave Konnie a helping hand. So if you are planning a Jedi feast, these should definitely be on your menu!

- 6 eating apples
- 25g unsalted butter (cut into cubes)
- 225g soft brown sugar
- 1 tablespoon golden syrup
- 5 tablespoons water
- 1 teaspoon vinegar
- chocolate sprinkles
- lolly or chop sticks

1. Wash and dry the apples. Remove any stalks and push sticks into the core of each apple and then put them in a fridge to chill.

2. Put the butter, sugar, golden syrup, water and vinegar in a saucepan and heat. Stir gently until the sugar has dissolved. Turn up the heat, gently bringing the toffee mixture to the boil stirring continuously.

3. Keep cooking the mixture for around 15 minutes until it has turned clear. Carefully remove the pan from the heat and place on a heatproof mat. Drop half a teaspoon of the mixture into a cup of cold water and after a few seconds test to see if the toffee has set hard. If it's not quite set return the pan to the heat and cook for a few more minutes.

4 Remove the apples from the fridge and carefully hold the stick to dip each one in the toffee, twisting it round until it is well coated.

5 Repeat this process to get a good coating and then sprinkle on chocolate while the toffee is still sticky.

6 Stand each apple on a tray lined with baking paper until the toffee has set. Allow the apples to cool before eating.

Konnie xxx

Blue Peter

42

Konnie Huq

My day as a dinner lady all started after I'd been watching tv and reading newspapers full of bad publicity about the quality of school dinners. I suggested that it might be very interesting to find out what being a good dinner lady is all about.

My trainer was expert Jeanette Orrey, who has spent years campaigning for better quality school dinners. Jeanette teaches dinner ladies from all over Britain to prepare meals which are tasty, healthy and not too expensive as all schools have to work on a strict budget. For instance, during my training, Jeanette told me off for using too much cheese in a recipe. She explained that even a few too many extra grammes could blow the budget and get the dinner lady into trouble.

My challenge was to come up with a menu which children would want to eat, which would taste delicious and which the school could afford. After a lot of thought and talking to some of my potential customers, the children of St Peter's Primary school in Nottinghamshire, I discovered that chips were a top favourite. Unfortunately, they are also high in fat and not that good for you and as I wanted food that was delicious and nutritious, I eventually decided on chicken meatballs with pasta twirls and crunchy vegetable bake, with carrot cake for afters. I joined St Peter's team of dinner ladies to get it all ready. We had just three hours and in what seemed like no time, I was behind the counter, serving up my creations. They were steaming hot and smelt fantastic.

After I'd loaded up the very last plate, I joined some of the children to see if they'd liked what I'd cooked for them. I'm delighted to say the answer was yes and the sea of empty plates seemed to prove that no-one was just being polite. I had been given a fascinating and exhausting glimpse into what it takes to do a really important job well.

Blue **Peter**

LAND OF THE

It took 12 hours to fly from London to Tokyo, Japan's capital city and the first destination on our summer expedition. If you're wondering why we were all wearing face masks, the reason is that the Japanese are very polite people. The idea of the masks, which we saw everywhere, is simple – you keep your germs to yourself!

Both the past and the future are very important throughout Japan. The Maiko are the ultimate traditional gentlewomen of Japan. They follow a strict training regime to become graceful, elegant and respectful, painting their faces white to show their purity. Once the elaborate costume and make-up went on, at least I began to look the part but I was glad I didn't have to face the years of hard work it takes to become a real Maiko.

Alongside the skyscrapers and shopping malls in Japanese cities, you regularly come across temples and shrines, many hundreds of years old. We took time out at this Buddhist temple to meditate and escape from the pressure of modern life, in our case a very busy filming schedule.

Blue Peter

RISING SUN

We visited the Toei film studios, where thousands of top Japanese films and tv shows are made each year. We had been invited to take part in a live, stunt-packed show in which I would play a Ninja warrior squaring up against Geth as the Ninja's arch enemy, the Samurai.

We were both amazed by the transformation and Konnie and Zoe watched spellbound as we leapt about, trying to live up to the fierce pride of these ancient warriors and their traditions.

After all that action, we found the perfect way to unwind – in an Onsen or bathing pool. For centuries, the Japanese have favoured the healing properties of relaxing in hot, natural springs full of minerals which bubble up from deep below the earth's surface.

It's not only humans who enjoy the miraculous powers of the natural Onsen – we visited a colony of Japanese snow monkeys who take the plunge every afternoon.

The Japanese are theme park crazy. We visited one of the oldest, Fujuku High Land, home to Japan's highest roller coaster. It was the ultimate white-knuckle ride, especially for poor Geth who really hates them.

It was meeting the people of Japan that I enjoyed most. Over half the villagers of Ogimi are over 80 and many are over 100. The secret of their long life and happiness? This lady told me it was keeping active and drinking sake, a strong traditional drink made from rice.

If keeping active is good for you, then 10-year-old Manae must be super-healthy. I was exhausted after the day I spent with her, a day crammed with lessons, sport, music, dance and karate. As I set off to collapse in our hotel, Manae had just started her homework.

Blue Peter

In Kyoto, I was challenged to master another ancient Japanese martial art – kendo. It is a bit like fencing. You use a bamboo pole called a shinai to score points against your opponent. To be any good, you must have speed, stamina and concentration. I did my best but to be honest, my opponent had nothing to worry about.

When we went out for an evening of Karaoke (which means 'empty orchestra') it turned into one of the best nights of our trip, although our singing was enthusiastic rather than tuneful!

Japan is an endlessly fascinating country. During the four fantastic weeks we spent filming our reports from the Land of the Rising Sun, every day was different and all of us hope one day to return.

No Oil Painting

"Hey Geth!" came the voice on the 'phone. It was the boss. "Any objections to being turned into a living painting?"

"None at all," I replied, thinking that it sounded interesting and that at least it wasn't going to be another of those tough physical challenges which were brilliant but could be painful.

How wrong I was and talk about suffering for your art! What I didn't realise was that top body painting artist Emma Cammack needed a blank canvas and in my case that meant my hairy chest had to go. Konnie and Liz sprang this news on me during a live show. They'd thoughtfully had a few hours training in chest waxing but all I can say is, I wish they'd had a bit more. I tried to be brave about it but it really was agony and I honestly have no idea why top sportsmen like David Beckham and Gavin Henson are fans of the treatment.

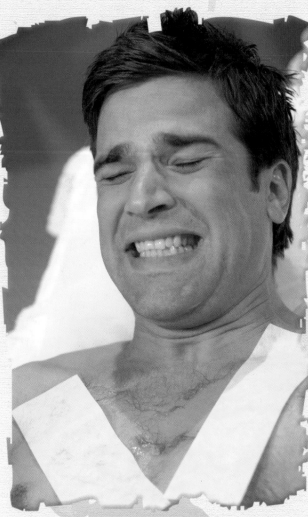

The painful bit over, on our next programme, Emma got to work. The process took most of the day and I had to hide in make-up during my few short breaks.

Emma used an airbrush to cover the large areas and a paint brush for the finer details. I was to be camouflaged into a pop art painting. Her inspiration came from the animal world where many creatures from stick insects and chameleons, to lizards and zebras are able to blend themselves into their surroundings to escape predators or sneak up on their prey.

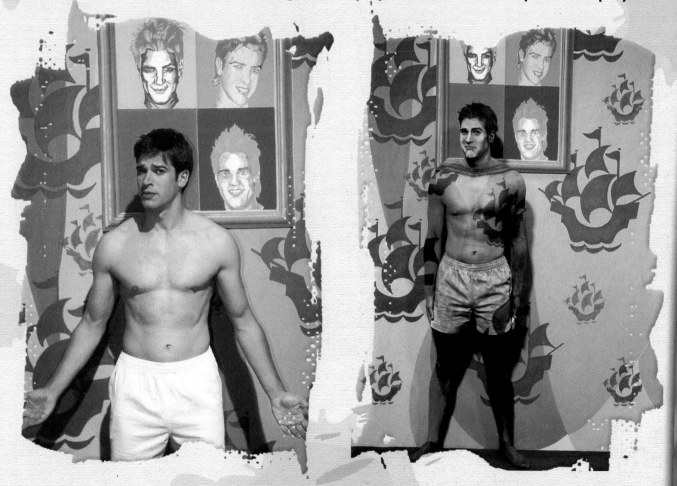

I must say I was staggered when I compared the before and after. Emma had turned me into a work of art. To be honest, though, I'm not sure I'd do it again because no-one told me that as soon as my chest had been waxed smooth, the hair would start re-growing. A slow and seriously itchy process!

SMACKDOWN

GET READY TO
RUMBLE WITH
OUR WRESTLING
RING FOR YOUR
FAVOURITE
ACTION FIGURES

1 To make a wrestling ring you will need an empty pizza box. Tape closed the open side or lid and this will become the floor of the ring.

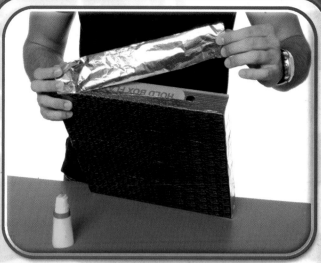

2 Cover the top of the box with sticky-backed plastic and decorate the 4 edges with silver tape or aluminium foil.

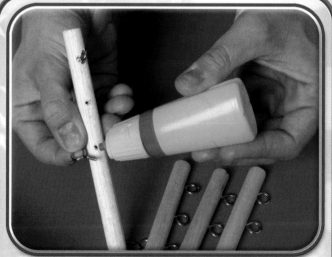

3 The 4 corner posts are made from pieces of thin dowelling. Each post is 17 cm long and the ends need a light rub with sandpaper to remove any sharp edges. Mark 3 positions on each post for the screw eyes which hold the ropes in place. The first mark should be 2 cm from the top, the second 3 cm lower and the third 3 cm lower down again. Dab each screw eye with a little glue before twisting them into the marks on the post.

4 To slot the posts into the ring, use a bradawl or sharp pencil to make a small hole in each corner of the wrestling ring floor. When the holes are just about big enough, dab a little glue on one end and push each post neatly into place. Make sure the posts are vertical and allow the glue to dry.

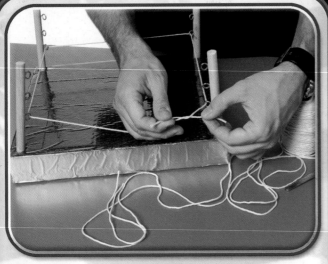

 String ropes are essential for the wrestlers to bounce off. Thread 3 rows of string through the screw holes and tie all the knots in one corner.

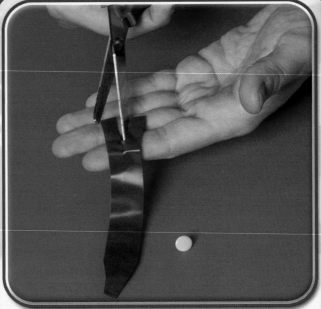

 The posts need padding so the wrestlers don't get KO'd. Cut a 25 cm length of coloured tape and fold almost in half lengthways leaving 3 cm of tape uncovered. Snip the folded end into a point and slit the sticky end up the middle.

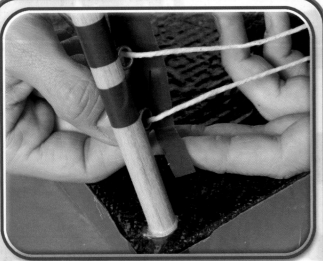

Use a drawing pin to attach the pointed end of the tape to the post and separate the other end so the tape wraps around the post facing inside the ring. Do this on all the posts.

 If you want to take your wresting ring a step further make a cage from a large cardboard box to fit over the pizza box. Cut away one side completely and measure 3 cm around each edge of the remaining 3 sides. Cut out the inner rectangles on each side. Paint the frame with dark grey paint. Measure and mark each edge of the box at 2 cm intervals. Using a bradawl or point of a pencil carefully make a hole on each mark.

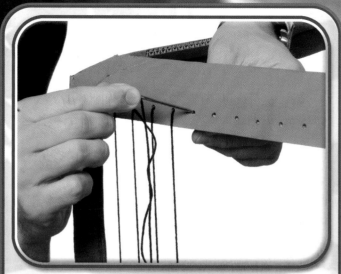

Thread a darning needle (which has a large eye) with a long length of black wool – twice the length of the box to be on the safe side. Push the needle through the first hole on the bottom of the box and take it up to the corresponding top hole, pushing the needle in and through the hole next to it. Pull the wool taut and continue working up and down until the whole side is covered with vertical lines of wool.

 **10**

Repeat the pattern working horizontally to create a netting effect. Do the same on the 3 remaining sides of the box but leave the top and bottom open.

 **11**

The lights are made from plastic lids from milk or fruit juice bottles. Cut out a cross shape from silver card and trim the edges so they slope out slightly. Put some glue in the centre of each lid and push the piece of card in the middle and it will look like the "barn doors" on professional lights. Attach the finished lights to the sides of the roof of the cage.

Now just add your wrestling figures and let battle commence.

What not to wear...?

In the world of fashion ideas are constantly recycled but as we discovered some have stood the test of time better than others....

Back in the swinging 1960s, the mini-skirt was magic and they've been in and out of fashion ever since. In the 1960s, designers experimented with funky new fabrics like plastic and metal which was all very groovy but not very comfortable. Unless I was going to a Sixties-themed party, I don't think I'd go out in this one.

As for my groovy colourful kaftan, worn with floppy hat and lots of beads, this was another popular 60s look but not one I'd pop on for a trip to the supermarket because, well...people would stare!

They call the 1970s "the decade that taste forgot" and I think these clothes are just disgusting. Clumpy platform shoes and boots were all the rage and they could seriously damage your health. There were reports of broken ankles and even legs from dedicated trend-setters who took a trip in them.

In the early 1970s, from the tight tops to the flared trousers, colours clashed and the materials used were often hot and uncomfortable. Zoe is wearing "hot pants" which hit the headlines in 1971 and really didn't suit many people. And just check out the size of my collar. It was a very hairy time too – beards and moustaches for the boys and long hair for both sexes, kept in style with lots of hairspray (which was very bad for the environment).

Blue Peter

By the mid-1970s, disco fever had arrived in Britain and the king of disco was Hollywood superstar John Travolta. Thousands of men copied this look, which Travolta wore in the film Saturday Night Fever. The cream suit might have looked smart but it was very sweaty to wear on the dancefloor and as for the medallion worn with the open-necked shirt, this soon became a joke and not a craze likely to return in a hurry.

In the 1980s, fashion got physical but instead of bright-coloured lycra staying in the gym, it hit the streets too. Leg-warmers, usually worn by dancers, were everywhere (ask your Mums and Dads) and looked, frankly, pretty stupid. Except maybe on dancers!

The 1980s wasn't for the fashion faint-hearted. I'm modelling the "new romantic" look but I'm not in love with it one little bit. Make-up and big hair on men isn't for me. Just too much trouble and if I turned up for tea at my Mum's house looking like this, she'd have a fit.

Meanwhile, I'm trying another 80s craze – power-dressing. Everything you wore was supposed to create an impact and make you feel powerful. But this puffball skirt makes walking a challenge and again, I thought the overall effect was more embarrassing than powerful. I couldn't wait to get it back on the hanger!

As the 80s became the 90s, people still dressed to impress but now there were a whole new set of mistakes to make. For instance, as I come from Cardiff, not New York and my idea of rapping is what you do around Christmas time, this 'street style' just doesn't work on me.

I particularly hated my bum bag, fine for collecting change in a car boot sale but hardly an object of beauty and I had to agree with Zoe about her cycling shorts. Why would anyone want to wear them off the saddle?

Even the famously fashionable don't always get it right. Footballing legend and gold Blue Peter badge-winning David Beckham caused a stir when he wore a sarong or skirt on holiday a few years back.

But one major rule of fashion is that what works on holiday rarely works back at home. I popped out of our studio down to the local high street to see how the sarong went down there. And if you like stares, pointing fingers and open laughter, why not give it a go yourself?

Fashion can be expensive and embarrassing but it can also be a lot of fun. Everybody on Blue Peter knows that I'm into clothes and so I suppose I shouldn't have been that surprised when I was challenged to design three outfits to be modelled on the catwalk in a top London fashion show. I was given two weeks and a budget of £2000 to buy the materials I'd need and to have my designs made up by a professional dressmaker.

I thought hard about a theme for my creations. Inspired by Blue Peter's connections with the sea, I came up with 'Starfish', a maritime collection. Catwalk shows often feature really outrageous styles, designed to stand out from the crowd and create a buzz around their designer and I was determined to be as creative as possible and really let my ideas flow.

On the day of the show, I was a bundle of nerves. I'd lived, breathed and dreamed about my three outfits for days and days now. They were a shell-coloured sequin jumpsuit, with rope detailing, a sailor suit with a cropped jacket, rope belt and fastenings and what I hoped would be my showstopper – a dress of stunning blue organza on a mermaid theme.

Top designer Ben de Lisi gave me his verdict – although he hated the sailor suit, he pronounced the mermaid dress "beautiful" and said that if he was to give me marks, he'd go for seven out of ten. The show was packed. Konnie and I had front-row seats. As our models paraded down the catwalk in my creations, I felt a tremendous surge of pride. It really was a dream come true.

WHO•

Russell T. Davies is something of a genius. He's the man who brought Doctor Who back to life after many years off the screen and did it so successfully that it's now just about the most popular drama series made by the BBC.

Russell is also a fan of Blue Peter and when he popped in to see us, suggesting we might like to run a competition for our viewers to design a monster in the new series, we didn't think twice. All our big competitions need a brilliant prize and this was one of the best. Russell promised that the Blue Peter monster would form the basis of an entire episode. In fact, to make sure there was no chance of it being pushed into the background, he promised to write the episode himself.

We launched the competition in the middle of summer and to be honest, we were a little bit worried. During the summer so many people are away or out that television audiences tend to be at their lowest. But we needn't have worried. The entries arrived in their thousands and by the closing date we'd received 43, 920. Every single one was studied and it was obvious that Blue Peter viewers are not only big fans of Doctor Who, they also have pretty active imaginations when it comes to dreaming up scary monsters!

PETER

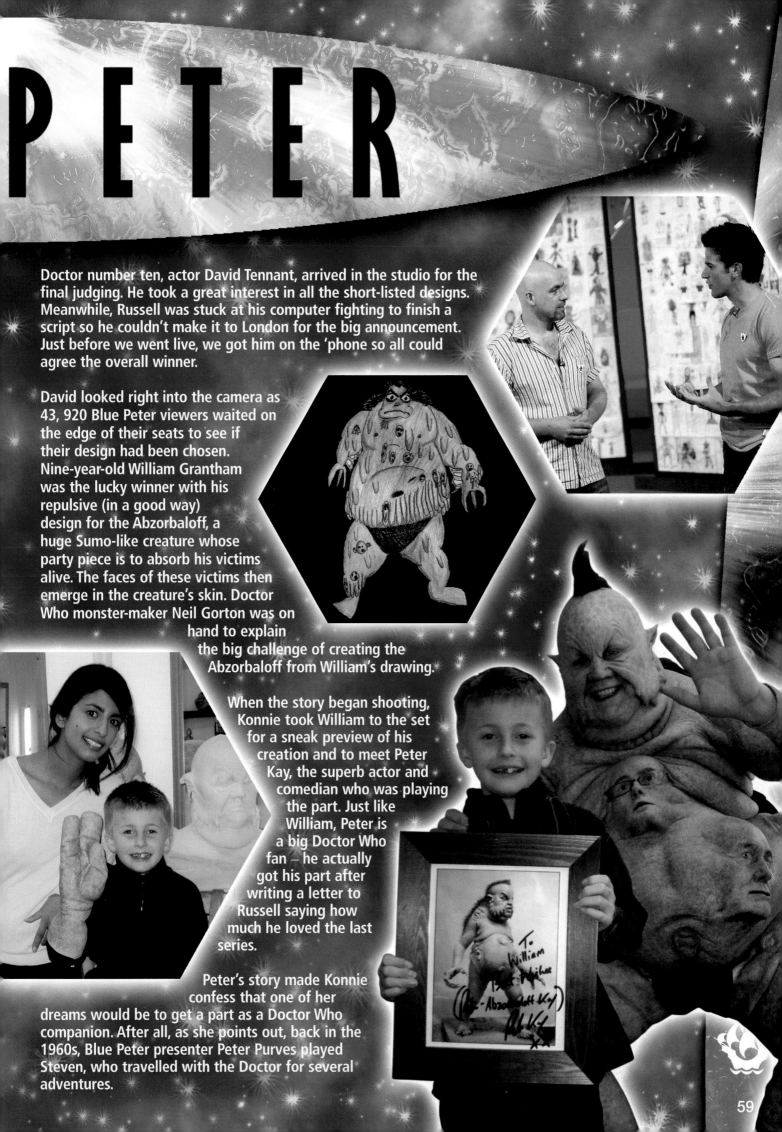

Doctor number ten, actor David Tennant, arrived in the studio for the final judging. He took a great interest in all the short-listed designs. Meanwhile, Russell was stuck at his computer fighting to finish a script so he couldn't make it to London for the big announcement. Just before we went live, we got him on the 'phone so all could agree the overall winner.

David looked right into the camera as 43, 920 Blue Peter viewers waited on the edge of their seats to see if their design had been chosen. Nine-year-old William Grantham was the lucky winner with his repulsive (in a good way) design for the Abzorbaloff, a huge Sumo-like creature whose party piece is to absorb his victims alive. The faces of these victims then emerge in the creature's skin. Doctor Who monster-maker Neil Gorton was on hand to explain the big challenge of creating the Abzorbaloff from William's drawing.

When the story began shooting, Konnie took William to the set for a sneak preview of his creation and to meet Peter Kay, the superb actor and comedian who was playing the part. Just like William, Peter is a big Doctor Who fan – he actually got his part after writing a letter to Russell saying how much he loved the last series.

Peter's story made Konnie confess that one of her dreams would be to get a part as a Doctor Who companion. After all, as she points out, back in the 1960s, Blue Peter presenter Peter Purves played Steven, who travelled with the Doctor for several adventures.

59

The Abzorbaloff wasn't the end of our Doctor Who connection this year. Liz's first job after leaving us was to present CBBC's Totally Doctor Who. Then, as well as the Dalek pen pot we showed on the programme and which you can find on page 62, we showed you how to create your own TARDIS too.

Then I had my own close encounter with the Time Lord when I travelled home to Cardiff, where Doctor Who is filmed, to play the part of a Cyberman. Cybermen are terrifying metal monsters who are part-human, part-machine. My biggest difficulty was actually getting into the Cyberman suit. They all have to be a standard size so they look absolutely identical but I was just a bit bigger and broader than the actor whose place I was taking. By learning how to half-breathe and not even think about claustrophobia, I managed it. But it was really difficult and I left the set with huge admiration for the actors who bring the monsters alive week after week.

Back in our studio, we met some other famous Doctor Who characters, Sarah Jane Smith (played by actress Lis Sladen) and her robot dog K9. Sarah had travelled with the Doctor back in the 1970s and she appeared in more episodes than any other companion. Russell decided to bring her back as he thought it would be interesting to see what happened when a companion from the past met a companion of today. Lis, who plays Sarah, says that making Doctor Who has changed a lot since her time but that it is still a labour of love and very hard work.

K9 was a gift from the Doctor to Sarah and the robot dog and his mistress have had their own adventures together. There may be more still to come – who knows? In the meantime, our dogs didn't quite know what to make of K9. I wondered if K9 might take part in one of our Bark In The Park sponsored dog walks in aid of the 75th birthday of Guide Dogs. There was a whirring sound and his ears clicked. "Affirmative, Gethin" came the reply.

When you think about it, Doctor Who and Blue Peter have a lot in common. Dogs, monsters, adventures, travelling companions and above all, in both programmes, the fact that you never quite know what to expect next.

61

E-X-T-E-R-M-I-N-A-T-E !
E-X-T-E-R-M-I-N-A-T-E !

Even a Time Lord needs somewhere to keep pens and pencils safe, so how about one of the galaxy's most frightening monsters to keep a beady eye on your possessions? A Dalek like this one will be sure to keep aliens at bay until the Tardis materialises and Doctor Who lands to stop an invasion of your pen pot.

If you want to construct your own Dalek you will need some earthly materials:

- 2 large yoghurt or soup pots with lids
- 1 crisps tube
- 1 plastic ball
- 1 cardboard egg box
- corrugated cardboard
- card and kitchen paper
- modelling clay
- cocktail sticks
- bendy straws
- beads
- sticky tape & black insulating tape
- glue & paint

1 To make the Dalek's body, cut 2 cm off the bottom of one of the soup pots and, with the lid in place, turn it upside down. Cut the crisps tube down to a height of 15 cm keeping the base intact.

2 Place the crisps tube inside the pot and secure the two together by wrapping sticky tape around the top.
To enlarge the base of the Dalek's body cut a strip of corrugated cardboard long enough to fit around it. Snip along one edge and tape the unsnipped half around the base. The snipped half can then be folded into the body where it narrows.

3 The Dalek's body is armour-plated. Use modelling clay to roll out a thin sausage shape and cut this into equal pieces.
Roll each one into a ball and then cut them into halves.
Glue them in lines of 4 down the body. Our Dalek had 10 rows around its body.

4 The head is made from a plastic ball cut in half and a second soup pot cut down to 7.5 cm. Use sticky tape to attach the section of ball to the pot. Cover the head with torn up pieces of kitchen paper which will smooth out the join and make a better painting surface.

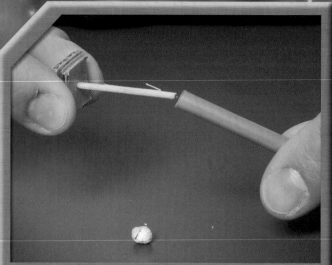

5 One of the Dalek's weapons is made from a cocktail stick and 2 squares of card one slightly bigger than the other. Push the cocktail stick into the smaller square of card and glue it onto the second square. Cover the cocktail stick with a length of drinking straw and push a little modelling clay or paper in the end. Glue the weapon in place.

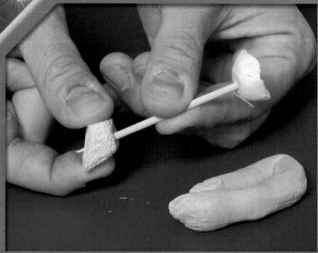

6 Push a cocktail stick into the piece of eggbox and cover it with a bendy section of straw. For the other end, make a cup shape from modelling clay or another piece of eggbox. Glue the finished weapon in place beside the other. Paint the plunger black

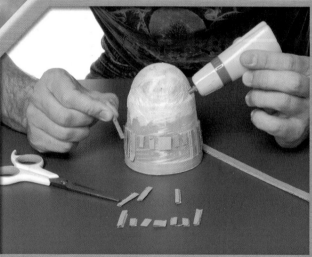

7 The panels above the Dalek's middle are strips of cardboard 3 cm long and 1cm wide. Glue the strips vertically all the way around and cut slightly shorter sections to fit above the weapons.

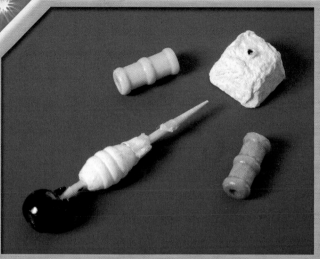

8 The Dalek's eye is made from one black and one white bead plus a tiny section of egg box threaded onto a cocktail stick. Glue everything in place before pushing the cocktail stick into the head. The ears are tubular-shaped beads stuck on either side of the eye. You could use short sections of drinking straw instead of beads.

9 Paint the Dalek's head and body in gold or silver and leave to dry. Decorate the base of the Dalek with black electrical tape.

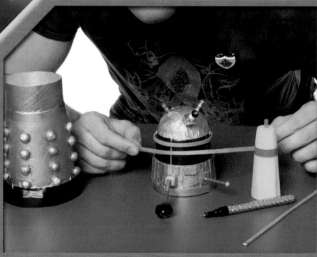

10 Use more tape to decorate the head section above the weapons. This should look like a grille so use a metallic marker pen to draw 6 vertical lines on the tape. Then cut 3 narrow strips of cardboard, paint them and then glue in place around the taped section.

11 Load up the body with pens and pencils, put the head in place and your Dalek is ready for action.

AN EIFFEL

Blue **Peter**

Paris is one of Europe's most exciting cities. It is only a couple of hours from the UK by 'plane or train and I have lots of happy memories of family holidays here. When I heard this was going to be Gethin's very first visit to this magical place, I knew we were in for a special trip.

The Eiffel Tower is the symbol of the city and wherever you are, it dominates the skyline. It is named after the man who built it – Gustave Eiffel. When he first presented his plans for the tower, he was asked if he was sure it would work. "Probably not," he replied, "But it will be fun to try…"

It was opened on May 15th 1889 and ever since, crowds have flocked to climb it.

There was a lot to fit in and our first stop was Monmartre, where many famous artists like Van Gogh, Renoir and Picasso lived and worked. The artists there today mostly draw quick cartoons of the tourists and we couldn't resist the 30 Euro asking price. What do you think of the results? We thought they weren't bad for a ten-minute sitting!

Everywhere you go in Paris, you see this game – boules – being played by the roadside. It is a bit like a combination of bowling and snooker and it's a fun and relaxing way of spending a few hours with friends.

We weren't here just to see the sights. I'd been given an amazing chance to take part in a show, performing that uniquely French dance, the Can Can. After just a few hours' rehearsal, I took to the stage. The routine flew past and although I loved every moment of it, I was completely exhausted too.

Gethin, meanwhile, had his own challenges. The first was to model the fashion the French are famous for. These are a couple of the looks I selected for him. They'd look a bit out of place in the Blue Peter studio but on the stylish streets of Paris, nobody batted an eyelid.

His second challenge was to help bake these – croissants. No Parisian breakfast is complete without them, although when Geth told me how much butter goes into giving them their gorgeous flavour, I decided that from now on, one was enough!

Blue Peter

We met up again to explore subterranean Paris. There are 21,000 km of sewers under the city and 150 years ago, poor families used to live down here. It must have been a grim experience, especially without electricity to illuminate the dark, smelly tunnels. The nearby catacombs are even older. They were originally Roman quarries. Then in the 19th century, when the Paris graveyards began to fill, bodies had to be removed to make room for new ones. They were brought here – and today you can walk for hours in dim, chilly corridors surrounded by an incredible six million skeletons. It is strange to think the skeletons were all once living, breathing, thinking people just like us.

The same is true when you look at what is probably the world's most famous portrait, Leonardo da Vinci's Mona Lisa.

Nobody knows who she was but her image has fascinated people for centuries. We were given special permission to film the picture when the museum in which it is housed, the Louvre, was closed. What struck me most was that the colours were actually quite muddy – perhaps not that surprising when you consider it is over 500 years old. Gethin liked her little smirk!

Disneyland Paris was one of the highlights of my visits to Paris as a child, even though I never got to meet Mickey Mouse! We'd been invited to the popular theme park to test a brand-new Space Mountain ride and take part in the famous daily character parade. I loved every minute of the ride.

Unfortunately Geth hates rollercoasters. I say unfortunately because to get all the shots we needed for the film, we had to go on it five times. It was a small consolation that the director, who'd volunteered to ride just behind us for moral support, lost his favourite hat in the third time round!

The parade was a wonderful way to finish our visit. We were playing sweeps on the Mary Poppins float and they take the whole thing so seriously we weren't allowed to wear our Blue Peter badges in case it spoilt the illusion for the crowds.

Our "Eiffel" of Paris rushed past. When we were waiting at the airport to fly home, I asked Gethin if he'd ever return. He grinned. "Mais oui, naturellement!"

Blue Peter

Marie Antoinette

This is me in the fabulous palace of Versailles, just a short drive from Paris and the glittering home of the Kings and Queens of France. Perhaps the most famous of these Kings and Queens was Marie Antoinette, who lived here just over 200 years ago. Marie was young and attractive when she became Queen and she hated the stuffy, pompous French court with its endless rules and regulations.

She spent her days – and several fortunes – amusing herself and leading fashion. She had so many dresses, she couldn't possibly remember them all, so a special book was made with samples from each one. Every morning, she'd look through the book and stick pins in the samples of the dresses she wanted to wear that day.

Thanks to her, elaborate artificial hairstyles became all the rage. Towering ever higher, these ridiculous creations must have been very heavy and uncomfortable, as well as distinctly unhygienic with some of them becoming the nesting ground for mice!

While the people in Paris grumbled about their extravagant Queen, Marie hid herself away at Versailles with her close friends and family.

Next, she set a new fashion – for all things simple, abandoning rich silks and satins and over-the-top hair styles. But Marie Antoinette's version of the simple life – complete with a toy village and miniature palace close to Versailles – still cost a fortune and caused gossip and scandal.

At last, in 1789, there was a revolution. The royal family became the prisoners of their people and were taken from Versailles to Paris. Marie's son, the heir to the throne, was dragged from her and the revolutionaries treated him with dreadful cruelty, deliberately turning him against his mother. Day after day, she could hear him crying but could do nothing to comfort him. She spent ages pressed up against the bars of her cell, hoping for a glimpse of him but he was never returned to her.

Soon her husband the King was tried and executed and then it was Marie's turn. She was sentenced to death by guillotine – a terrible machine invented to cut off its victims' heads. Before she died, aged just 37, she wrote one last letter in her filthy cell, so different from the luxury in which she had lived most of her life. "My deepest regret is having to abandon my poor children. You know that I only lived on for them."

Back in our studio, Madame Tussauds lent us their waxwork figures of Marie and her family – modelled from life – and these grisly death masks of the King and Queen. It is strange to think that in France today Marie Antoinette is still talked about and remembered, not as a villain but as a heroine – perhaps because of the extraordinary bravery she showed in those last terrible years of her life.

Socks

Our last cat Smudge was only on the programme for a year before his tragic death in August 2005. He was run over whilst out playing near his home. The news was a terrible shock and reached us just too late for the last annual. We all felt that we didn't want to replace him at once but as the weeks went past, the studio felt strangely empty without a feline friend.

On January 4th 2006, we felt the moment had come to introduce the 8th Blue Peter cat to viewers. We wanted a breed which would feel really at home in our studio and our expert friends at the National Cat Club suggested the Ragdoll. Ragdolls are pedigree cats who originated in America in the 1960s before arriving in Britain around 20 years ago. Typically, they are calm and gentle and love human company – perfect for our studio.

Paws for thought in our make-up room

Socks soon got on top of the cameras we use in the studio

Rocks!

A tiny kitten with a big future

The perfect way to relax before a live show

Lucy loved Socks from the minute they first met

Our latest feline superstar, a blue mitted ragdoll, was born on 30th September 2005, one of a litter of four kittens. As ever, we asked Blue Peter viewers to come up with the right name for him and we were staggered by the huge range you sent in – 52,294 of them in the end. 5200 of these suggested Socks.

Over time, we've been told that the contrast in Socks' fur will make his socks stand out all the more so we thought the name was purr-fect.

Socks soon settled into his new routine. On a busy programme with lots to pack in and all the nerves of a live transmission to think about, he stays as chilled as ever – and we all love him.

P.S. - Turn over for a great idea for a toy you can make for your cat or kitten.

Blue Peter

Feline Fun

If you want to make an octopus for your feline friend all you need is:

- an old pair of gloves
- string or wool
- coloured material
- cotton wool
- rubber bands

1 One of the gloves becomes the octopus body and when you put your hand inside you'll be able to wriggle the legs. It will really amuse your cat if there are tiny fish dangling on long pieces of wool. Cut 3 pieces of wool roughly 30cm long. Thread the wool onto a darning needle which has a large eye and tie a double knot in one end. Use the needle to thread the wool through a finger from inside the glove. Pull gently so the knot will keep the wool in place. Repeat with the remaining 2 lengths of wool.

2 To make tiny fish to tantalise your cat, cut out 3 squares of material roughly 9cm x 9 cm. Put a ball of cotton wool in the centre of each square, gather up the corners and use an elastic band to secure. The loose material will look a little like fish tails! To attach the fish, wrap the wool around the tail and tie securely.

3 To make a perfect octopus it needs three more legs. On the second glove, cut the thumb, little finger and wristband off. The remaining fingers will become the extra legs.

4 Push a little cotton wool into each leg and secure the cut end with an elastic band.

5 Use the middle part of the cut glove to make the head. Turn it inside out and bunch one end using an elastic band to secure. Turn it right sides out and fill with cotton wool.

6 Bunch up the opening and secure with another elastic band.

7 Glue or sew the 3 extra legs onto the octopus body and then sew the head on top which will disguise the untidy, bunched end on the extra legs.
To complete the octopus make eyes from 2 small circles of felt and glue in place.

Pop your hand inside the octopus and wriggle those fish in front of your cat. They're bound to love this toy just as much as Socks!

Treasure Trail

Every day, thousands of children struggling to cope with problems which range from bullying and abuse to dealing with divorce and loneliness 'phone ChildLine for advice or just for someone to talk to, someone who will really listen. All ChildLine counsellors are carefully trained to help these callers and the 'phone lines are open 24 hours-a-day. None of this comes cheap, however, and ChildLine has constant problems finding the money to keep it's work going.

That's why we decided to launch our Treasure Trail appeal. The treasure was stuff which nobody else wanted but which we knew we could turn into cash. Disused old and foreign currency and unwanted mobile 'phones, which could be sorted and recycled. We launched our Appeal by showing a series of real-life stories from ChildLine and we set our totaliser target to pay for 5,000 calls.

To say we were swamped by the reaction would be an understatement. Our message boards were buzzing and every day our inbox was full to bursting. The post came in sackloads. Yes, Blue Peter viewers knew all about the problems ChildLine were trying to help with and they were keen to join our Treasure Trail. As 11-year-old Blue Peter viewer Abbie Reid told us: "I know how much courage you need just to call that one number." Verity Dams, also 11, wrote: "I really like that you're trying to make a difference to so many children's lives."

Charlie Myers, aged 8, from Middlesborough, collected this heap of treasure after putting up posters in his school.

Amelia, Amy, Anna, Caroline and Oliver from Duxford School in Oxford did us proud.

Emma Raine, aged 12, from North Yorkshire and her table-load of treasure.

Cameron and Ewan Wilson, aged 9 and 6, from Hertfordshire, worked incredibly hard collecting 32 mobiles and over 2000 coins.

Richard from Gwent did well with his haul of treasure.

Charlotte and Emma Roberts, aged 11 and 7, combined carol singing with collecting and raised over £20.

On November 25th, just two weeks after launching our Appeal, we smashed the first target and encouraged by the response, we set a new target ten times bigger. On January 16th, we opened the programme with a colossal explosion as the 50,000 stage on our totaliser literally blew its top. It was a wonderful way to start the new year. Thanks to you, the exact number of calls we could now answer was 50,764.

By the time we went to press with this book, that figure had leapt to a staggering 146,764. Blue Peter viewers had done it again and exceeded our highest expectations.

It is a sad fact that the vital work that ChildLine will carry on as long as children have problems and feel that there is nowhere else for them to turn. But the Treasure Trail Appeal didn't just raise money to answer more calls, it helped people to realise that children of all kinds from all backgrounds often have very real problems which must be taken seriously. We'd like to say a huge "thank you" to everyone who took part.

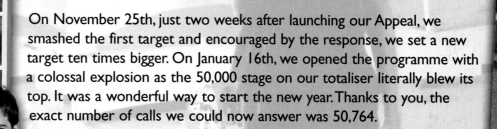

Blue Peter

Zöe

Blue Peter

Zoe Salmon

The minute I walked into the Blue Peter office I knew something was up. There was a buzz in the air.

"Morning Zoe!" came a cheery greeting from Nick Harris, one of our studio directors. Nick is a larger-than-life character who just loves directing big song and dance numbers. He was looking very pleased with himself. "Do you know the musical Grease at all?" "Know it?" I replied, "I love it. It's one of my all-time favourites." "That's good. Because we've got the cast of the new production coming in and for this performance only you're going to play Sandy and Gethin's going to play Danny."

I was so shocked I just took the CD and sheet music Nick offered me and went off to compare notes with Geth.

A few weeks later, we met the cast for a day's rehearsal. They couldn't have been more generous and helpful. When it came to the studio day itself, I'd almost forgotten that as well as the singing, the choreography and the costumes, we'd have to think about cameras too. But as soon as I heard those first familiar thudding beats of the Summer Nights track kick in, the music took over. Suddenley I wasn't Zoe from Belfast singing about Gethin from Cardiff. I was Sandy from Australia singing about Danny from America.

There really is no business like show business!

COMMANDO YOMP

I relish the challenges you face as a Blue Peter presenter but when I agreed to take part in the Royal Marines commando yomp, I had no idea just what I'd taken on.

To become a commando and win their much prized green beret, Royal Marine recruits have to pass a series of gruelling tests, the last and most arduous of which is a 30-mile 'yomp' (which means walking and running) across Dartmoor, carrying heavy equipment. It must be completed in less than eight hours.

I had just three months to train so I set off for the Royal Marines Commando Training Centre at Lympstone in Devon where I was kitted out and put through a series of physical tests to see just how much work I'd have to do. It was a tough day and made me realise I was going to need bucket-loads of fitness and courage if I was to be able to push my body to go beyond anything it had endured before.

From that moment on, I trained as often and as hard as I could, running with a weight on my back after studios and during filming trips. Days off were a thing of the past.

Blue Peter

The weeks soon passed and then it was back to Lympstone to take part in the final commando yomp. I felt like a very new boy when I settled into my bunk alongside the rest of Troop 891.

Just a few hours later, in the early hours of the morning, it was time to "crack on" as the Marines say. For the first six miles, I felt on top of the yomp, keeping up with the troop and singing the Welsh national anthem to keep me going. Then, slowly but surely, muscle fatigue began to set in, not surprising when you consider that the weight we were all carrying is the equivalent of about 35 bags of sugar. The pressure of this soon started to create blisters and sores.

Blue Peter

83

The only time we stopped were at the checkpoints along the route where we were given a few short minutes to eat a pasty and a banana for energy and grab a 'wet' or drink of water. I grew to hate the taste of those pasties but it was all there was and our bodies needed the fuel.

By now, it is no exaggeration to say that my muscles felt as if they were being ripped apart. I could no longer feel my feet at all. All that mattered was to keep going.

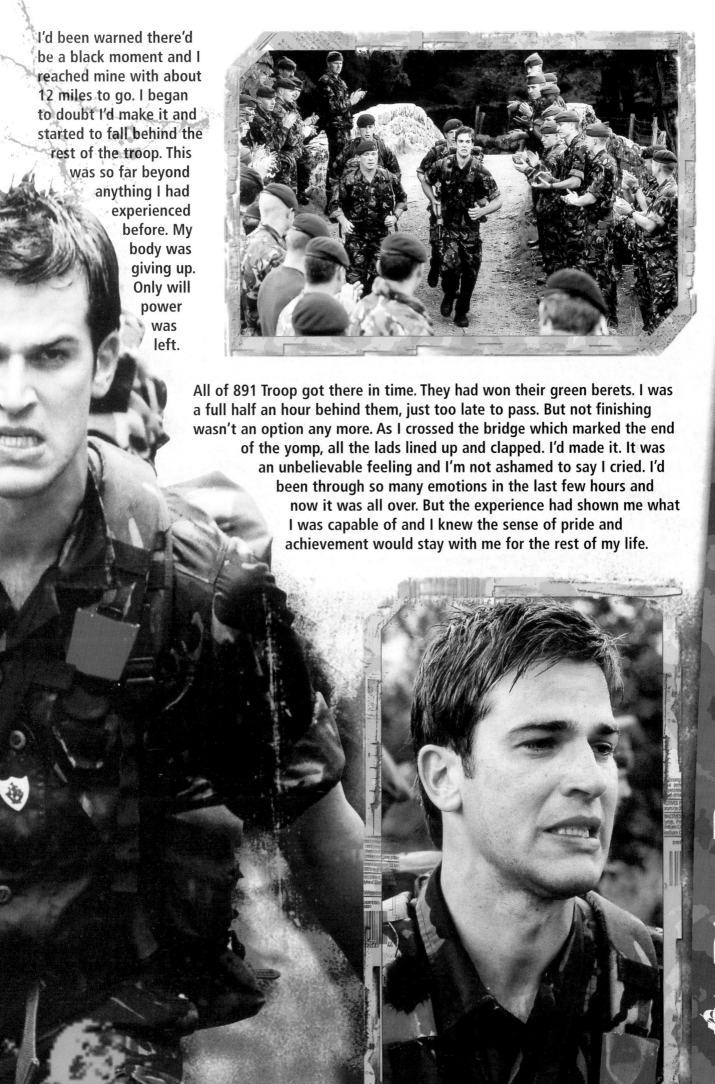

I'd been warned there'd be a black moment and I reached mine with about 12 miles to go. I began to doubt I'd make it and started to fall behind the rest of the troop. This was so far beyond anything I had experienced before. My body was giving up. Only will power was left.

All of 891 Troop got there in time. They had won their green berets. I was a full half an hour behind them, just too late to pass. But not finishing wasn't an option any more. As I crossed the bridge which marked the end of the yomp, all the lads lined up and clapped. I'd made it. It was an unbelievable feeling and I'm not ashamed to say I cried. I'd been through so many emotions in the last few hours and now it was all over. But the experience had shown me what I was capable of and I knew the sense of pride and achievement would stay with me for the rest of my life.

Blue Peter

Badge Winners

Every week thousands of emails and letters flood into the Blue Peter office. We love hearing from you and if you write an interesting letter, you could well win a badge or even end up on tv as the star of one of our badge hits, where we surprise viewers at home or in school. Plus, at the end of every programme, we always feature a star badge-winner and show their photo. If you get in touch and you're in luck, it could be you!

I am writing to you about my gardening. I decided to grow my favourite meal, which is salad. I grew some carrots, cucumbers and tomatoes and planted some peas saved from last year's crop. I like to eat these raw!
Love from
Josey Smith
Ceredigion, Wales

I really like Doctor Who. My hobby is making things. I hope you like what I have made. I am looking forward to seeing K9 in the new series. I'm going to make your Dalek.
Oak Macwilliam
Tattwnhall, Cheshire

We saw you making these blueberry muffins and wanted a go ourselves, so we tried it out and they were easy to make (with a bit of help!) and they were absolutely delicious!) We're looking forward to trying out some new ideas soon.
Indiana and Kai Lawrence
Thanet, Kent

Blue Peter

...saw you making these blueberry muffins and wanted a go...
...we tried it out and they were easy to make (with
...ately delicious. Here is a
...d to

I really enjoyed your programmes on Japan and I remembered our Round the World charity day at school. We had to come in dressed as people from anywhere in the world and I came in wearing a kimono. We raised over £300 for charity and donated some of it to Childline. I love your show!
Beth Price
Cheadle Hulme, Cheshire

...nue, mat, liz, zoe and simon,

...writing to tell you about the bluepeter

...oom I made a

...res of it.

bedsid...

...moolir

I entered your Shaun the Sheep competition and thought you might like to know about the other models I have been busy making. At the moment I am working on Wallace, Rocky and chick. I hope you enjoy looking at what I have made!
Peter Watson
Solihull

...Peter
...My like Doctor who

I saw you make the mobile 'phone holder so I decided to make one of my own. I used mosaic plastic shapes to make an A on the front of it. I already have a Blue badge, which I wear with pride. I'd love to have a silver one to go with it.
Annabelle Skilbeck
Thornton Cleveleys
Lancashire

Blue Peter

...zk Macwilliam
...(an

This is a photo of me just about to go up and down on a bungee trampoline. It was taken in Benidorm, Spain. I was terrified! The first jump I took was the worst but by the fourth, I was doing back flips in the air and I loved it!
Louis McLaughlin
Glasgow
Scotland

I grew vegetables in our garden last summer. We grew them organically so we had to kill the slugs by drowning them in beer! Hope you like my picture – please send me a green badge!
Jacob Bradbury
Southampton

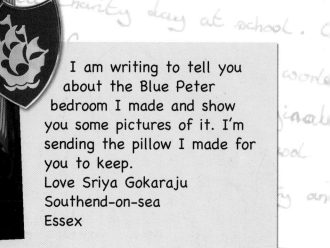

I am writing to tell you about the Blue Peter bedroom I made and show you some pictures of it. I'm sending the pillow I made for you to keep.
Love Sriya Gokaraju
Southend-on-sea
Essex

Blue Peter

88

Would you like to win a Blue Peter badge, as modelled here by some of our music makers? There's the blue, awarded for an interesting email or letter, a good idea for the programme, poem, picture or story. To win your silver, you have to do something different from whatever won you your blue. Green badges are awarded for anything environmental you've been involved in or written to us about. All runners-up in Blue Peter competitions win a competition winners' badge. We've just introduced a new version of these in a lovely orange colour. Gold badges are our highest award, given for outstanding achievements or bravery. The newest Blue Peter badge is purple in colour and you can win one if you get selected to join our Blue Peter team players. All the details about that are on our website.

Blue Peter badges famously give winners a great perk – free entry into many wonderful attractions across the UK. Sadly this year we were forced to temporarily suspend this privilege when it was revealed that some people were selling badges on the internet. Of course if you win a badge it is up to you what you do with it but we didn't think that it was fair to allow people who just buy a badge to get the free entry won by real badge winners. The story hit the headlines and tv news and there were even questions asked in Parliament about the badge cheating.

It was 11-year-old Blue Peter viewer Helen Jennings who came up with the solution. Helen wrote to us and said she was "too scared to wear my own blue badge in case people think I bought it off the internet." Helen suggested a badge card with the winners' signature and a hologram to prove they are entitled to free entry. We thought it was a great idea and from now on, badges will be sent with one of our new cards. The idea won Helen her silver badge. Now its over to you – which colour will you go for and how many badges can you win?

Blue Peter

music makers

Since Blue Peter started way back in 1958, there have only been seven versions of Barnacle Bill, our famous theme music. When we decided it was time to find the eighth we knew just who we wanted to mastermind it for us. Murray Gold is the very talented man who arranged the Dr Who theme, as well as composing the music for it and many other major films and tv shows. He was extremely busy but jumped at the chance, especially when we explained that this would be no ordinary job.

We knew from your emails and letters that many of you love music and we thought this might give us the chance to run a really ambitious competition. So, teaming up with our friends at BBC New Talent and the BBC Philharmonic Orchestra, we launched Blue Peter Music Makers, a UK-wide search to find 40 talented viewers to play alongside the Philharmonic on Murray's brand-new version of our theme. Before the recording session, all the players would spend three days at a Music Makers camp, rehearsing, hanging out and having fun. We weren't just looking for people with musical training either – a sense of rhythm and musicality could get you through.

A staggering 25, 639 viewers completed the online application form and from that, 500 were invited to audition in locations across Britain.

Blue Peter

It was phenomenally tough to whittle that 500 down to the chosen 40 but we managed it in the end and just before Easter, all of them plus Murray and the Music Makers experts and the entire Blue Peter team arrived for the start of what became a truly wonderful experience. When you think that many of the kids involved had never been away from home before, it was amazing there weren't more problems like homesickness, but each day flew past and everyone seemed to get on really well. On the last day, top conductor Alexander Shelley flew in from Germany to rehearse our Music Makers. He was impressed.

Early the next morning it was time to report to the BBC's big recording studio in Manchester for last-minute rehearsals. By mid-afternoon, families and friends had arrived to watch our Music Makers, now completely transformed in their smart concert clothes, record the final version of the theme. Everyone felt nervous. Tension was in the air. Murray, close to tears, welcomed everyone before Alexander took the stage, raised his baton and masterfully guided the orchestra – with their 40 highly-talented new recruits – through Murray's superb arrangement, an arrangement that from now on, you'll hear at the start of every Blue Peter programme and which for us will always bring back memories of a brilliant experience and some incredibly talented young people.

Happy Endings

My last day on Blue Peter was a really happy one. It's a tradition that no-one ever tells you what exactly is going to happen and although I'd asked for a programme with plenty of friends and family, I could never have guessed that so many special people would make the effort to turn up and wave me goodbye. I'd decided to leave after nearly six years because I was planning to move out of London with my husband and our son Dex and back to the Cambridgeshire countryside where I grew up. Blue Peter is a brilliant job but you can't do it by halves, so once we'd decided on the move, I knew my time was up.

So many special guests - what a send-off!

My gold badge - a real honour!

This crown was one of many wonderful cards and presents sent in by viewers.

Me and my boys - Dex and my husband Michael.

Being presented with a gold badge, the programme's highest award, was an extra special surprise, especially as it was given to me by one of the many viewers I'd awarded badges to over the years. Matt did a fantastic job of guiding me through my last show, helped by a giant book of memories which he presented to me right at the very end. Have a look at just a few of them, all of them moments I'll treasure forever.

I've just loved all the dressing up I've done. Here I am as a 1940s movie star, Vivien Leigh.

More dressing up, this time as Dee Dee in Totally Blue Peter. I really enjoy acting but when it comes to singing, I'm afraid I usually had to mime!

This costume was designed for me by a Blue Peter viewer.

I spent a few days as a sailor on HMS Illustrious and I was really homesick!

I've laughed a lot on Blue Peter. Usually at myself!

In our mini-serial The Quest I played the alien Princess Banana. She called herself Banana because her real name was too hard to pronounce.

Just three months later and it was my turn to move on, taking Meg with me. I cannot really believe it's the end for us. Leaving Blue Peter was certainly the toughest decision I've ever had to make and I know I'm really going to miss it. I just felt that after seven years and 727 programmes, I should bow out while I love the programme as much as I do. It has totally changed my life and given me opportunities that I'd never have dreamt were possible a few years ago. I'd like to say thank you to all the brilliant Blue Peter viewers who've been my mates through all my many challenges. Here's my pick of just a few of my many adventures.

I reported from Melbourne, Australia when the city hosted the World Gymnastics championships. I was a champion gymnast as a young lad so it was a real thrill.

In Russia, I joined the crew of the Standart and after a few hours hard graft, I smelt to high heaven!

From one extreme to another – in our Rock n'Roll Christmas I had to go from wimp to warrior under instruction from Aussie he-man Sam!

In The Quest I was taken over by the Gul, an evil alien intelligence which arrived on Earth during a cricket match.

It took three hours to transform me into Big Daddy, the character I played in one of our Christmas specials. I lost a lot of weight in that suit!

The sheepskin might look a bit silly but it at least it kept me a bit warmer during one of my coldest filming trips, recreating the horrors of life in a First World War trench

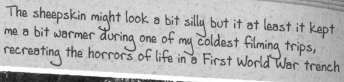

I'd never ridden before I joined Blue Peter. Over the last seven years, though, I've become really at home in the saddle. This was the day I spent playing the fast and furious game of polo. I managed to score!

I passed the Royal Marines potential recruits' course despite getting mixed up between my right and left when on parade.

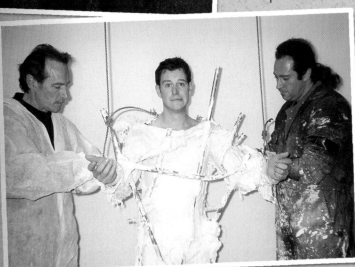

No time to develop an itch — this is me getting plastered so that the sculptors could turn me into a waxwork at the Jorvik Viking exhibition in York. I'm still on display — if you ever visit, see if you can spot me!

Fooling around during my filming trip to Isle of Man. I teamed my Manx kilt with my favourite boots — but they were a bit slippy on those rocks!

I'LL TRY ANYTHING ONCE

Flashback to January 5th 2005 and my very first Blue Peter. Looking back, it is all a bit of a blur but one incident is burnt into my memory. I was asked if I had anything I was scared of or that I wouldn't do. Cool as you like, I heard myself answer, "No, there's nothing I wouldn't do." I saw a slight reaction from the other presenters as I spoke but I didn't think much more about it. Until, that is, my new boss 'phoned me up full of excitement.

"What you said was genius," he said enthusiastically. "It really got us thinking in the office and you're going to love what we've come up with. A whole series of films for you. We're calling them 'I'll Try Anything Once'. They'll push you but that's what Blue Peter is all about. We'll do the first couple then wait for viewers to suggest some more."

It turned out that Blue Peter viewers were only too keen to come up with ways to test my nerve. Over the last few months I've tried everything from pot-holing to sewer cleaning. Here are a few of my favourite activities that I've tried once, starting with the day I took a leap of faith and went sky-diving for the first time.

Blue **Peter**

Launching myself off the end of Bognor Pier was sheer madness. I was taking part in a human-powered flight competition. I just sank but it was such good fun, I'd try it again!

After my day 'on the bins', I have new respect for the people who do this tough, dirty job, day after day.

Building an igloo was back-breaking enough but staying inside it overnight was hideous. It was so cold, sleep was virtually impossible.

Racing in this Formula One car was no hardship. In fact, it was a dream come true. Talk about adrenaline!

Learning to barefoot water-ski was so hard I cried. But when I cracked it, I felt over the moon.

Blue Peter

97

But they all pale by comparison with my biggest challenge this year – running the London Marathon. This was the moment in the studio when I found out I'd been entered. I was so excited I didn't stop to think about what it actually meant until a few hours later. Most people train for about six months to be in the right shape to run the gruelling 26 mile route. I had less than half that time. What was worse, an assessment by a physiotherapist revealed that partly because of years of dance training when I was growing up, my running style was all wrong and that unless I changed it, I'd almost certainly injure myself. Blue Peter arranged great support for me in the form of Team Zoe – nutritionist Matt Lovell, who would advise me on the right things to eat, and personal trainer Stuart Amory. Stuart is ex-RAF, Scots, tough as old boots and very supportive. They saw me all the way through my intensive training.

I had my setbacks, of course but I was really sustained by the fantastic support of Blue Peter viewers in the form of messages, emails, cards and letters. The day of the Marathon, 23rd April 2006, will live with me forever. Lining up at the starting point was an incredible feeling. There was just such a buzz in the air. I tried not to think about cameras, finishing times or worse still, not completing. I just took it one stage at a time. I'll not deny it was hard. Physically, it was the hardest thing I've ever done. But the feeling of crossing that finishing line made it all worthwhile. I'd set a target of just under 6 hours and managed to complete the course in five hours 31 minutes and 27 seconds. I was never going to break any records but I felt a real sense of achievement and I was proud to be the first-ever Blue Peter girl to run the world's most famous marathon.

P.S. And in case you're wondering, I'll still try anything once!

Peter

Happy Birthday Mabel

To star in one of Britain's top tv programmes for ten years is quite an achievement for anybody but it is especially remarkable when you realise that the star in question has four legs and a tail. What's even more remarkable is that it could all have turned out so differently.

Sadly, Mabel's first few months were marked by cruelty and neglect. She had been rescued by the Royal Society For the Prevention of Cruelty to Animals and was still just a puppy when Blue Peter decided to feature the wonderful work of the RSPCA. The RSPCA were looking to find someone who might provide Mabel the right home, with lots of love in it. At about the same time, we were looking for a new dog to join the programme and so Mabel and Blue Peter came together at just the right moment.

On 19th February 1996 RSCPA Inspector Mark Buggie drove our tail-wagging new recruit into Studio One at Television Centre and she joined the team. Mark explained why she was called Mabel. Because his initials were M.A.B. and her RSPCA kennel was marked M.A.B.1, the name Mabel had stuck. We thought it was perfect for her.

Since then Mabel has been a friend to twelve presenters and nine pets, not to mention literally millions of Blue Peter viewers. We were determined to celebrate her ten-year milestone in style and so we commissioned sculptor Ptolemy Elrington to make a special statue of Mabel for the Blue Peter garden. Ptolemy uses recycled materials and his Mabel was mostly made from old car hubcaps. We thought it was a great likeness – what do you think?

Of course Mabel took all the fuss in her stride as she has done all her hundreds of Blue Peter programmes. She may not be as young as she was but she still loves playing with a ball of any kind or having a romp round the garden or studio with her best friend, Lucy. Meeting Mabel all those years ago was a lucky day for her and Blue Peter. To us, she really is a dog in a million.

ANDY'S AUDITION

This is me having a last minute dab of powder before one of the most nerve-racking days of my life so far - my final Blue Peter audition. My journey to become the programme's 32nd presenter was fast and furious. I was working as a runner at CBBC. Runners are the most junior members of a television production team. As their name suggests, they fetch, carry and generally help out with anything and everything. My ambition was to make documentary films and I saw being a runner as my first step in that direction. That's when fate took over. After work one day, I'd joined a group of mates for a drink in the BBC Club. Little did I know it then but Blue Peter director Catherine Patterson heard me chatting and thought I might be just the person to join the team.

She popped her head round the door of Richard Marson, Blue Peter's Editor, and he asked me in for a chat. Several more chats followed and a whole series of different tests before Richard offered me the chance to audition in the Blue Peter studio. He told me it was vital to be myself, no matter what I was asked to do.

Easier said than done and there's no point in pretending that the studio audition is anything but terrifying. You present a complete mini Blue Peter but unlike the usual programmes where the presenters share the items, each one is presented by the auditionee. One hurdle is making a Christmas card. I don't think my robin turned out quite right!

The other presenters were really supportive as they knew just what I was going through. Here is Gethin lending me a hand when I was trying to demo a remote-controlled Dalek.

Cleaning Lucy's teeth with special beef-flavoured toothpaste for dogs was the easiest challenge because she was as good as gold.

It was tough knowing that up in the studio control room, Richard was watching my every move. I knew I was up against some fierce competition too.

I had done my best, and Richard asked me to come and see him at 1230 the next day. I didn't sleep much that night. But when I arrived, Richard grinned and said, "How would you like to join the team?"

What a bizarre week. On Monday I'd been a runner and by Friday I was off to make my very first film as Blue Peter's newest presenter.

Konnie told me that it was important I got stuck in, no matter how silly I felt. So when I was asked to have a go at belly dancing and impress the camera crew with my trampolining skills, I just grinned and went for it. It was surprisingly enjoyable!

NUMBER 10 DOWNING STREET IS THE MOST FAMOUS ADDRESS IN BRITAIN.

THE TOP TEN

IT IS HERE THAT THE GOVERNMENT MAKE ALL THEIR DECISIONS, DECISIONS WHICH AFFECT EACH ONE OF US. AS A HIGH SECURITY BUILDING IT ISN'T OPEN TO THE PUBLIC SO WHEN PRIME MINISTER TONY BLAIR INVITED ME TO TAKE A LOOK INSIDE, I MADE SURE I TOOK BLUE PETER CAMERAS WITH ME.

The Prime Minister was hard at work when I arrived and he suggested I took a tour before we met up for a chat.

The walls of the sweeping main staircase are lined with pictures of every British Prime Minister, 51 of them so far and all in order of when they lived and worked here.

I loved the beautiful state room where the Prime Minister welcomes important guests – everyone from Nelson Mandela and President Bush to little Ant and Dec!

When the Prime Minister holds a state banquet, this is where the lucky V.I.P's have their dinner.

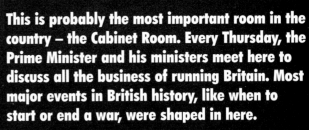

This is probably the most important room in the country – the Cabinet Room. Every Thursday, the Prime Minister and his ministers meet here to discuss all the business of running Britain. Most major events in British history, like when to start or end a war, were shaped in here.

Mr Blair knew all about Blue Peter and when he was a boy used to try some of our makes. Although he enjoys cooking, he told me that his children don't think much of his efforts. His favourite recipe is spaghetti bolognese. After our chat, the Prime Minister waved me goodbye.

Number 10 is one of the most extraordinary houses in the land and I feel very lucky to have been given the chance to explore it.

Eggs-travaganza!

It doesn't have to be Easter to make and give these beautiful, colourful eggs with their hidden surprise.

You will need 2 plastic pudding basins to begin making an exquisite Easter egg.

If you like the zig-zag ribbon pattern, start by marking 4 holes at equal distances apart around the bottom of both basins. Make another 4 marks around the top of each basin just under the rim. These marks should be in between those at the base and also at equal distances apart.

Use a bradawl or skewer to make the holes where the marks are but be very careful. If you find it tricky then ask an adult to help.

Paint the outside of each basin including the rims with enamel or acrylic paint. Do it a little at a time and use a piece of cloth to gently blot over the paint so you end up with a mottled effect.

Decorate the egg in contrasting coloured ribbon or string – anything you can lay your hands on. If you wrap a little sticky tape around the end of the ribbon or string it will be easy to thread through the holes, making a zig zag pattern until you have gone all the way around. Use sticky tape to fasten the ribbon ends to the inside of the egg.

5

To make the egg look even more decorative, push paper fasteners through the holes or cover them with pretty shaped stickers. Glue jewels in the spaces in between the ribbon. Buttons or beads also look attractive.

6

Create a tiny handle by painting a large button or bead and glueing it in place on top of the egg.

7

The bottom half of the egg needs to be weighted by putting a large lump of modelling clay in the base. Cut a circle of card or use an old plastic lid to cover the clay.

Fill the rest of the base with shredded tissue which makes a nice soft place to nestle small chocolate eggs. Finally put the two halves together and put it on display or give the luxury egg to someone as a really special present.

Solutions & Credits

Our address is:
Blue Peter
BBC TV Centre
London W12 7RJ

Our home page is:
Online: http://www.bbc.co.uk/cbbc/bluepeter
Email: bluepeter@bbc.co.uk

Written by Richard Marson

Co-Ordinator: Anne Dixon

All makes by Gillian Shearing, except Feline Fun
by Diggy Hicks-Little

Illustrations by Bob Broomfield
Photography by Chris Capstick

Other photographs by:
Jon Applegate, Mignon Aylen, Matt Baker,
Alf Batchelor, Bridget Caldwell, Matt Day,
Tim Fransham, Matt Gyves, Adrian Homeshaw,
Gethin Jones, Richard Kendal, Alex Leger,
Richard Marson, Ross Millard, Rob Norman,
Ros Sewell, Squeeze Photography, Ed Willson.

If we have left anyone out, we are sorry!

The author would like to thank Sarah Courtice and
the Blue Peter team for their help and ideas. Every
effort has been made to contact copyright holders
for permission to reproduce material in this book.
If any material has been used without permission,
please contact us.

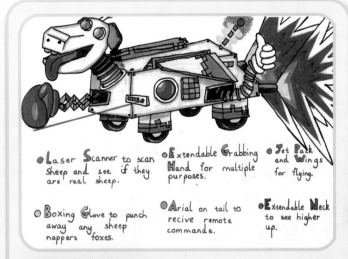

- **Laser Scanner** to scan sheep and see if they are real sheep.
- **Extendable Grabbing Hand** for multiple purposes.
- **Jet Pack and Wings** for flying.
- **Boxing Glove** to punch away any sheep nappers foxes.
- **Arial on tail** to recive remote commands.
- **Extendable Neck** to see higher up.

This is the design which won 11-year-old Bradley Lord top prize in our competition to design a character for Nick Park's Shaun The Sheep series. Bradley came first out of a whopping 47,268 entries. Nick and the judges loved his idea for a robot sheepdog.

HELLO THERE! PICTURE SOLUTIONS

1. For National Poetry Day, I played war poet Wilfred Owen, one of the young men who wrote poems to express the appalling suffering they witnessed during the horrors of the First World War.

2. The studio gave 13-year-old Liam Mower a standing ovation when he visited us to perform one of his high-energy dance numbers from the multi-award winning West End musical Billy Elliot.

3. "Am I bovvered?" I suppose I should have known better than to offer teenage tearaway Catherine Tate one of our badges for appearing in the studio.

4. Joining the BBC Symphony Chorus to sing in the world-famous Last Night of the Proms was an unforgettable experience. Here I am, giving my all to the rousing anthem Land of Hope and Glory, the climax of the show and of the entire Proms season.

5. Back in the summer, the legendary statue of Lord Nelson had two faces – his own and mine after I'd climbed this world-famous London landmark to help with a special clean and repair operation.

6. Gold badge and Oscar-winning animator Nick Park actually animated a few seconds of exclusive footage for us in a mini Blue Peter studio on the day we launched our record-breaking Shaun the Sheep competition.

7. In a studio far, far away….Mabel and Lucy didn't seem at all bothered when we transformed ourselves into characters from the Star Wars films. May the Force be with us!

8. We welcomed back our old friend, ex-presenter Simon Thomas, or to be more accurate, he surprised us with a fantastic practical joke during CBBC's half-term comedy week. We went through an entire item about a bizarre character called Alphonse (Simon in heavy disguise) with his "theatre of the body" before Simon took off his mask and revealed that the whole thing was a clever hoax.

9. Don't try this at home – those bricks were about to shatter everywhere. The spectacular Shaolin Monks had us on the edge of their seats with a stunning performance which combined dancing and ancient martial arts.

10. It's a miracle that I'm all smiles in this picture. It was taken after I'd stood at attention for two hours outside Television Centre to see if I was up to the standards of the elite Welsh Guards who regularly complete the same feat of endurance outside Buckingham Palace. Try it yourself sometime. It is no joke!

11. When Will Young used computer wizardry to put himself into vintage Blue Peter clips for the video to his single Who Am I?, I was given exclusive behind-the-scenes access and a cameo part.

12. He just made it into this book – meet Blue Peter's brand new and 32nd presenter Andy Akinwolere, who took over from Matt and whom you'll be getting to know very well over the next few months.